Presented to

_____

From

_____

Date

_____

God's Little
Devotional Book
for Students

An Imprint of Cook Communications Ministries
Colorado Springs, Colorado

Introduction

Every student faces the big questions of life: Who am I? Why am I here? What's life all about? God's Little Devotional Book for Students helps answer those serious questions—but in a way that is fun to read, and which fits into today's busy lifestyle.

Each of the devotionals is linked to a quote—some familiar, some new—and also to a passage from the Bible. The illustrations and stories are ones that will cause you to think, and in some cases, to laugh, to cry, to remember. The devotionals build upon a foundation of what is good, right, hopeful, loving, and moral—a foundation that was firm not only in times past, but in today's world. The entries in this book are both timely, and timeless. And because they are linked to the truth of God's Word, the meanings they convey are eternal!

God's Little Devotional Book for Students helps build you up on the inside. The devotionals are designed to bolster excellence of character and strength of integrity. They provide encouragement and give evidence for faith.

The title may say "Little Devotional Book" because the devotionals are short in length, but big in meaning!

God's Little
Devotional Book
for Students

When you were born, you cried and the world rejoiced.
Live your life in such a manner that when
you die the world cries and you rejoice.

A painting in an ancient temple depicts a king forging a chain from his crown, and nearby, another scene shows a slave converting his chain into a crown. Underneath the painting is this inscription: "Life is what one makes it, no matter of what it is made."

You may have been given certain "ingredients," just as a baker may find the staples of flour, sugar, and oil in his kitchen; but what you create from the talents and genetic propensities given you is up to you. Live your life so that it might be measured according to these words of an anonymous poet:

Not—How did he die? But—How did he live?
Not—Where did he gain? But—What did he give?

These are the units to measure the worth
Of a man as a man, regardless of birth.
Not—What was his station? But—Had he
a heart?
And—How did he play with his God-
given part?
Was he ever ready with a word of good cheer,
To bring back a smile, to banish a tear?
Not—What was his shrine? Nor—What was
his creed?
But—Had he befriended those really in
need?
Not—What did the sketch in the news-
paper say?
But—How many were sorry when he
passed away?

The memory of the righteous
will be a blessing.
PROVERBS 10:7 NIV

After haggling heatedly for several hours about which type of water main to purchase for their city, the town council of Pacific Vista was still deadlocked. One member suggested, "Let's appoint a committee to confer with the city engineer at Los Angeles to find out which type they have found to be most successful over the years. If we can profit by another city's mistakes, I think we should do so."

Leaping to his feet, an angry councilman—obviously full of civic pride but with little discretion—replied, pounding his fist on the table, "Why should we have to profit by the mistakes of Los Angeles? Gentlemen, I contend that Pacific Vista is a big enough town now to make its own mistakes!"

> Many receive advice; only the wise profit by it.

Most of us are surrounded by good advice at any given time.

The books of our libraries are full of it.

Preachers proclaim it weekly.

People with highly varied experiences and backgrounds abound with it.

Schools give access to it; labs report it.

Commentators and columnists gush with it.

But all the good advice in the world is worth very little if it isn't heeded. Be one of the wise—value and apply it!

Pride only breeds quarrels, but wisdom
is found in those who take advice.
PROVERBS 13:10 NIV

> ### Even a mosquito doesn't get a slap on the back until it starts to work.

Many people know how Helen Keller overcame the difficult physical challenge of being rendered deaf, dumb, and blind after a fever as a baby and how she eventually learned to communicate, learning Braille. Her life inspired millions—one of her ardent admirers being Mark Twain. She was invited to visit every U.S. President at the White House from her childhood on.

What many people don't know, however, is how hard Helen worked as an adult. After graduating with honors from Radcliffe College, she worked to help others until her death at the age of eighty-eight. She wrote numerous articles. She gave lectures for the American Foundation for the Blind, and she helped raise a fund of some $2 million for this foundation. On her eightieth birthday, the American Foundation for Overseas Blind honored her by announcing the Helen Keller International Award for those who gave outstanding help to the blind.

We are not only called to overcome our own faults, weaknesses, and limitations, but we are asked to exercise our strengths. "Just surviving" isn't what we are challenged to do. We are destined to use our talents for God's purposes, putting all our minds, hearts, and energy to the work He sets before us.

Work hard so God can say to you,
"Well done." Be a good workman,
one who does not need to be ashamed
when God examines your work.
2 TIMOTHY 2:15 TLB

When Ruth Bell was a teenager, she was sent from her childhood home in China to school in Korea. At the time, she fully intended to follow in her parents' footsteps and become a missionary. She envisioned herself a confirmed "old maid" ministering to the people of Tibet. While at school, however, Ruth did give some serious thought to the kind of husband that she might consider. As she tells in her book A Time for Remembering, she listed these particulars:

"If I marry: He must be so tall that when he is on his knees, as one has said, he reaches all the way to heaven. His shoulders must be broad enough to bear the burden of a family. His lips must be strong enough to smile, firm enough to say no, and tender enough to kiss. Love must be so deep that it takes its stand in Christ and so

> You will never make a more important decision than the person you marry.

wide that it takes the whole lost world in. He must be active enough to save souls. He must be big enough to be gentle and great enough to be thoughtful. His arms must be strong enough to carry a little child."

Ruth Bell never did become a full-time missionary in Tibet. However, she did find a man worth marrying: Billy Graham. As his wife, Ruth Bell Graham became a missionary to the whole world!

Therefore shall a man leave his father and his mother, and shall cleave unto his wife: and they shall be one flesh.

GENESIS 2:24

15

The Bible has a word to describe "safe" sex: It's called marriage.

The 1960s were known for many rebellions, among them the sexual revolution. "Free love" spilled from the hippie movement into the mainstream American culture. Premarital sex relations sanctioned by the "new morality" became openly flaunted.

One of the unexpected results of this trend, however, received little publicity. As reported by Dr. Francis Braceland, past president of the American Psychiatric Association and editor of the American Journal of Psychiatry, an increasing number of young people were admitted to mental hospitals! In discussing this finding at a National Methodist Convocation on Medicine and Theology, Braceland concluded, "A more lenient attitude on campus about premarital sex experience has imposed stresses on some college women severe enough to cause emotional breakdown."

Looking back over the years since the "new morality" was sanctioned by a high percentage of the American culture, one finds a rising number of rapes, abortions, divorces, premarital pregnancies, single-family homes, and cases of sexually transmitted diseases—including herpes and HIV. The evidence is compelling: the old morality produced safer, healthier, and happier people.

Marriage should be honored by all,
and the marriage bed kept pure,
for God will judge the adulterer
and all the sexually immoral.
HEBREWS 13:4 NIV

Charles Oakley, forward for the New York Knicks and an NBA All-Star, has a reputation for being one of basketball's best rebounders. It's his toughness, however, that has probably contributed the most to his outstanding sports career.

While other professional players seem to have frequent injuries, or are sidelined for other reasons, Oakley hasn't missed a game in three years, even though he has absorbed a great deal of physical punishment. He is often pushed, or fouled. He puts in miles each game running up and down the court. He frequently dives into the stands for loose balls, to the extent the courtside media teases him about being a real working hazard. According to Oakley, his

No horse gets anywhere until he is harnessed. No life ever grows great until it is focused, dedicated, disciplined.

tenacity and energy have a source: his grandfather Julius Moss.

Moss was a farmer in Alabama who did most of his fieldwork by hand. "Other people had more equipment than he did," Oakley says. "He didn't have a tractor, but he got the work done. No excuses." Moss, who died five years ago, developed all sorts of aches and pains in his life, but he laughed at them and went about his business. Oakley saw a lesson in that—nothing should prevent him from earning a day's pay.

Being focused, dedicated, and disciplined will make the difference between a mediocre life and a great life.

In a race, everyone runs but only one person gets first prize . . . to win the contest you must deny yourselves many things that would keep you from doing your best.

1 CORINTHIANS 9:24-25 TLB

I have never been hurt by anything I didn't say.

A young attorney, just out of law school and beginning his first day on the job, sat down in the comfort of his brand-new office with a great sigh of satisfaction. He had worked long and hard to savor such a moment. Then, noticing a prospective client coming toward his door, he frantically searched for his legal pad. Uncapping his pen, he picked up the telephone. Cradling it under his chin, he began to write furiously as he said, "Look, Harry, about that amalgamation deal. I think I better run down to the factory and handle it personally. Yes. No. I don't think $3 million will swing it. We better have Smith from Los Angeles meet us there. OK. Call you back later."

Hanging up the phone, he put down his pen, looked up at his visitor, stood, extended his hand, and said in his most polite but confident lawyer voice, "Good morning. And how might I help you?"

The prospective client replied, "Actually, I'm just here to hook up your phone."

> Many a foible or flaw
> Need not show . . . for
> If you don't say so,
> Others won't know!

Don't talk so much. You keep putting your foot in your mouth. Be sensible and turn off the flow!
PROVERBS 10:19 TLB

One day a boy at summer camp received a box of cookies from his mother. He ate a few, then placed the box under his bed. The next day he discovered the cookies were gone.

Later, a counselor, who had been told of the theft, saw a boy sitting behind a tree eating the stolen cookies. He sought out the victim and said, "Bill, I know who stole your cookies. Will you help me teach him a lesson?" The boy replied, "Well, I guess—but aren't you going to punish him?"

The counselor said, "Not directly—that would only make him hate you.

> We too often love things and use people, when we should be using things and loving people.

I have an idea. But first I want you to ask your mother to send some more cookies." The boy did as the counselor asked and a few days later another cookie parcel arrived.

The counselor then said, "The boy who stole your cookies is by the lake. I suggest you go down there and share your cookies with him." The boy protested, "But he's the one who stole from me!" "I know," said the counselor. "Let's see what happens."

An hour later the counselor saw the boys come up the hill—the thief earnestly trying to get his new friend to accept his compass in payment for the stolen cookies, and the victim just as adamantly refusing, saying a few old cookies didn't matter all that much!

Be devoted to one another in brotherly love.
Honor one another above yourselves.
ROMANS 12:10 NIV

> One hundred years from now it won't matter if you got that big break, or finally traded up to a Mercedes. . . .
> It will greatly matter, one hundred years from now, that you made a commitment to Jesus Christ.

"Richard Cory," perhaps Edwin Arlington Robinson's most famous poem, is a good reminder never to judge the state of a man's heart by the size of his wallet or the grandeur of his possessions:

Whenever Richard Cory went down town,
We people on the pavement looked at him:
He was a gentleman from sole to crown,
Clean favored, and imperially slim.
And he was always quietly arrayed,
And he was always human when he talked;
But still he fluttered pulses when he said,
"Good-morning," and he glittered when he walked.
And he was rich—yes, richer than a king—
And admirably schooled in every grace:

24

In fine, we thought that he was everything
To make us wish that we were in his place.
So on we worked, and waited for the light,
And went without the meat, and cursed
the bread;
And Richard Cory, one calm summer night,
Went home and put a bullet through his head.

It's only when Christ is the only One who ultimately matters, that everything else matters!

What is a man profited, if he shall gain
the whole world, and lose his own soul?

MATTHEW 16:26

In both fall and spring, geese often can be seen migrating, flying in a beautiful V-shaped formation. Such a pattern may appear to us to be a thing of beauty. In fact, it is aerodynamically brilliant.

At certain intervals, relative to the strength of the headwind they are encountering, the lead goose—who does the most work by breaking the force of wind—drops back and flies at the end of the formation. A goose next in the V takes its place. Scientists who have studied the V-formation have calculated that it takes up to 60 percent

> Success is knowing the difference between cornering people and getting them in your corner.

less effort for the geese to fly this way. The flapping of wings creates an uplift of air, an effect that is greater at the rear of the formation. In essence, the geese are taking turns "uplifting" one another. After a turn at the point of the

V, the lead goose is allowed to rest and be "carried" by the others until it has an opportunity to regain its strength, move forward in the formation, and eventually take its place in the lead role again.

How fortunate we are when we are part of a circle of friends and family who cooperate and work together. All are "lifted up" when that happens. Is there someone today you can "uplift" in prayer, giving, or heart-to-heart friendship and caring?

Can two walk together,
except they be agreed?
AMOS 3:3

> Shoot for the moon.
> Even if you miss it you
> will land among the stars.

A young man who was disconcerted about the uncertainty of his future and in a quandary as to which direction to take with his life, sat in a park, watching squirrels scamper among the trees. Suddenly, a squirrel jumped from one high tree to another. It appeared to be aiming for a limb so far out of reach that the leap looked like suicide. As the young man had anticipated, the squirrel missed its mark— but, it landed, safe and unconcerned, on a branch several feet lower. Then it climbed to its goal and all was well.

An old man sitting on the other end of the bench occupied by the young man remarked, "Funny, I've seen hundreds of 'em jump like that, especially when there are dogs around and they can't come down to the ground. A lot of 'em miss, but I've never seen any hurt in trying." Then he chuckled and added, "I guess they've got to risk it if they don't want to spend their lives in one tree."

The young man thought, A squirrel takes a chance—have I less nerve than a squirrel? He made up his mind in that moment to take the risk he had been thinking about . . . and sure enough, he landed safely, in a position higher than he had even dared to imagine.

Aim for perfection.
2 CORINTHIANS 13:11 NIV

Helping the deaf to communicate was Alexander Graham Bell's motivation for his lifework, perhaps because his mother and wife were both deaf. "If I can make a deaf-mute talk," Bell said, "I can make metal talk." For five frustrating and impoverished years, he experimented with a variety of materials in an effort to make a metal disk that, vibrating in response to sound, could reproduce those sounds and send them over an electrified wire.

The secret of success is to do the common things uncommonly well.

During a visit to Washington, D.C., he called on Joseph Henry, a scientist who was a pioneer in research related to electricity. He presented his ideas to him and asked his advice—should he let someone else perfect the telephone or should he do it himself. Henry encouraged him to do it himself. When Bell complained that he lacked the necessary knowledge of electricity, Henry's brief answer was, "Get it."

And so Bell studied electricity. A year later when he obtained a patent for the telephone, the Patent Office officials credited him with knowing more about electricity than all the other inventors combined.

Hard work. Study. Hope. Persistence. These are all "common things." They are the keys, however, to doing uncommonly well.

Seest thou a man diligent in his business?
he shall stand before kings; he shall
not stand before mean men.
PROVERBS 22:29

Definition of status: Buying something you don't need with money you don't have to impress people you don't like.

Guy de Maupassant's The Necklace is the story of a young woman, Mathilde, who desires desperately to be accepted into high society. One day her husband, an ordinary man, is given an invitation to an elegant ball. Mathilde borrows a necklace from a wealthy friend to wear to the occasion. During the course of the evening she receives many compliments from the aristrocracy present, but she also loses the necklace.

In order to restore the lost jewelry, Mathilde's husband borrows 36,000 francs, tapping every resource available to him. A look-alike necklace is created and Mathilde gives it to her friend, telling her nothing of what happened.

For ten years, the couple slaves to pay back the borrowed francs, each of them working two jobs. They are forced to sell their home and live in a slum. When the debt is finally cleared, Mathilde sees her well-to-do friend one day. She confesses that the necklace she returned was not the one she borrowed, and she learns: the necklace loaned to her had been made of fake gemstones! The borrowed necklace had been worth less than 500 francs.

Trying to "keep up appearances" is often a way ultimately to lose face.

They do all their deeds to
be noticed by men.
MATTHEW 23:5 NASB

A man once took his three-year-old daughter to an amusement park. It was her first visit to such a place and she was in awe at all the sights and sounds, but mostly she was thrilled at the whirl and whiz of the rides. She insisted on one particular ride, even though it was considered the "scariest" ride for children her age.

As she whipped around the corners in her kiddy car, she wrinkled up her face and let loose with a terrified cry. Her father, riding in the car with her, got her attention. With a big smile, he shouted over the roar of the ride, "This is fun!" When the little girl saw that he was not terrified, she also began to laugh. The new experience that had turned terrifying suddenly became enjoyable. In fact, she insisted on riding the same attraction three more times.

> I like the dreams of the future better than the history of the past.

What a comfort it is to know that our Heavenly Father will not only "ride the new ride" with us, but that the future is never scary to Him. He has good things planned for us. When we look into the future from our perspective, we may become frightened. But when we look at the future from His perspective, we are far more likely to shout with glee, "Let's go! Isn't this going to be fun!"

Remember ye not the former things,
neither consider the things of old.
Behold, I will do a new thing.
Isaiah 43:18-19

> ## The way to get to the top is
> ## to get off your bottom.

In the fall of 1894, Guglielmo retreated to his room on the third floor. All summer while on vacation, he had read books and filled notebooks with squiggly diagrams. Now, the time had come to work.

Every day, he rose early. He worked all day and long into the night, to the point that his mother became alarmed. He had never been a robust person, but now he was becoming appallingly thin. His face was drawn, and his eyes were often glazed over with fatigue. Finally, the day came when he announced his instruments were ready. He invited the family to his room and, pushing a button, he succeeded in ringing a bell on the first floor! While his mother was amazed, his father was not. He saw no use in being able to send a signal so short a distance. So, Guglielmo labored on. Little by little, he made changes in his sending circuits so he could send a signal from one hill to the next, and then beyond the hill. And, eventually, his invention was perfected—partly by inspiration, but mostly by perseverance.

Guglielmo Marconi was eventually hailed as the inventor of wireless telegraphy, radio's forerunner. He not only received a Nobel prize in physics, but a seat in the Italian senate and the title of marchese.

How long will you lie down, O sluggard?
When will you arise from your sleep?
PROVERBS 6:9 NASB

Joe Smith was a loyal carpenter who worked nearly two decades for a very successful contractor. The contractor called him into his office one day and said, "Joe, I'm putting you in charge of the next house we build. I want you to order all the materials and oversee the job from the ground up." Joe accepted the assignment with great enthusiasm. He studied the blueprints and checked every measurement and specification. Suddenly, he had a thought: If I am really in charge, why couldn't I cut a few corners, use less expensive materials, and put the extra money in my pocket? Who will know? Once the house is painted, it will look great.

You are only what you are when no one is looking.

So Joe set about his scheme. He ordered second-grade lumber and inexpensive concrete, put in cheap wiring, and cut every corner he could. When the home was finished, the contractor came to see it.

"What a fine job you have done!" he said. "You have been such a faithful carpenter to me all these years that I have decided to show you my gratitude by giving to you as a gift this very house which you have built."

Build well today. You will have to live with the reputation you create.

Not with eye-service, as men-pleasers;
but as the servants of Christ, doing
the will of God from the heart.
EPHESIANS 6:6

There are times when silence is golden; other times it is just plain yellow.

According to an old fable, three men once decided to engage in the ascetic practice of absolute silence. They mutually agreed to keep a "day of quiet" from dawn until the stroke of midnight, at which time a full moon was expected to rise from the horizon. They sat cross-legged for hours, concentrating on the distant horizon, eager for darkness to envelop them.

One of them unwittingly noted, "It's difficult not to say anything at all."

The second one replied, "Quiet. You're speaking during the time of silence!"

The third man sighed and then boasted, "Now I'm the only one who hasn't spoken yet."

A rap singer has "updated" some of the advice given by the book of Ecclesiastes to add these lines:

"There's a time to speak up . . . and a time to shut up.

"There's a time to hunker down . . . and a time to go downtown.

"There's a time to talk . . . and a time to walk.

"There's a time to be mellow . . . and a time not to be yellow.

Silence can be good, but never if it's the result of raw fear or lack of moral fiber.

To every thing there is a season . . . a time to keep silence, and a time to speak.
ECCLESIASTES 3:1-7

Marie and Pierre Curie's marriage was based on love and admiration, but their scientific partnership was based on hard work. Marie often had to move heavy containers, using an iron bar almost as big as she was to empty the contents of one container into another, perspiring as she stirred fuming caldrons of liquid in hopes of separating out materials usable for their experiments. She insisted a strict work discipline be kept, and she established rigorous laboratory customs for herself and their assistants. Every night, the bench tops were to be left clean. The lab atmosphere was to be quiet.

Keep thy shop and thy shop will keep thee.

In 1896, they began studying the emitted rays from uranium salts—a phenomenon Marie called radioactivity—and in 1898, the

Curies discovered polonium. Their work began to pay off handsomely. In 1903, she and Pierre shared the Nobel prize in physics with Henry Becquerel for their investigations of uranium and radioactive materials. When Pierre was killed in a tragic accident on the streets of Paris, Marie continued their work, becoming the first woman to teach at the Sorbonne. In 1911 she won a second Nobel prize, this time in chemistry.

The "shop" Marie Curie kept so diligently certainly rewarded her!

He who works his land will have abundant food, but he who chases fantasies lacks judgement.
PROVERBS 12:11 NIV

Long ago, a band of minstrels lived in a faraway land. They traveled from town to town singing and playing their music in hopes of making a living. They had not been doing well financially, however. Times were hard and the common people had little money to spend on concerts, even though their fee was small.

The group met one evening to discuss their plight. "I see no reason for opening tonight," one said. "It's snowing, and no one will come out on a night like this." Another said, "I agree. Last night we performed for just a handful. Even fewer will come tonight."

The leader of the troupe responded, "I know you are discouraged. I am too. But we have a responsibility to those who might come. We will go on and we will do the best job of which we are capable. It is not the fault of those who come that others do not. They should not be punished with less than our best."

Heartened by his words, the minstrels gave their best performance ever. After the show, the old man called his troupe to him again. In his hand was a note, handed to him by one of the audience members just before the doors closed behind him. Slowly the man read, "Thank you for your beautiful performance." It was signed simply, "Your King."

Daniel was preferred above the presidents and princes, because an excellent spirit was in him.
DANIEL 6:3

For years, Arthur Blessitt has carried a 6-by-10-foot, 80-pound cross on his shoulders through towns and cities around the world. "It blows people's minds," he says. Once he has gained people's attention, he finds he has a unique opportunity to share the Gospel.

Blessitt first became well-known for preaching to hippies on Hollywood's Sunset Strip. He gained national attention when he undertook a cross-carrying journey—along with four members of his rock group, the Eternal Rush—to Washington, D.C. The 3,500-mile trip took seven months to complete. As the group traveled, they held rallies. Blessitt urged fellow Christians to meet him at the Washington Monument at the end of his trip—but not with empty hands. "Christians need to come and

The best things in life are <u>not</u> free.

give something," he preached. He asked that people bring or send two gifts for the nation's needy, gifts given openly with "both hands." Those who went to the capital to meet him found a third opportunity to give with an "open heart"—at a bloodmobile parked on the site.

While the Gospel may be "free" to all who receive it, the giving of the Gospel costs, and continues to cost, a great deal.

Ye were not redeemed with corruptible things, as silver and gold . . . but with the precious blood of Christ, as of a lamb without blemish and without spot.
1 PETER 1:18-19

> # You can lead a boy to college,
> # but you cannot make him think.

At Princeton, Woodrow Wilson was first a teacher and later, president of the university. While popular, he had a reputation for cracking down on students who were not serious in their pursuit of an education.

The mother of one young man who was expelled for cheating made a trip to Princeton to talk with Wilson. She pleaded with him to reinstate her son because of the possible adverse reaction his expulsion would have on her own health and reputation. She told him of an impending operation and she felt certain she would die if her son were not readmitted. Wilson heard her pleas and then responded, taking a very tough stance, "Madam, you force me to say a hard thing. If I had to choose between your life or my life or anybody's life and the good of this college, I should choose the good of the college."

Failure to study, and to apply oneself fully to one's studies, is a form of rebellion. The same holds for cheating. Do your best in school. Don't blame a teacher for being too hard on you, when the blame actually lies in your being too easy on yourself!

It is senseless to pay tuition to educate a rebel who has no heart for truth.
PROVERBS 17:16 TLB

In an extensive opinion survey, *The Day America Told the Truth,* James Patterson and Peter Kim reported some startling findings:

Only 13 percent saw all Ten Commandments as binding and relevant.

Ninety-one percent lied regularly, both at work and home.

Most workers admitted to goofing off an average of seven hours a week.

About half of the workforce admitted they regularly called in sick even when they felt well.

> If a man cannot be a Christian in the place where he is, he cannot be a Christian anywhere.

When they were asked what they would be willing to do for $10 million, 25 percent said they would abandon their families, 23 percent would be prostitutes for a week, and 7 percent would murder a stranger!

Lest you conclude that those surveyed were all ungodly criminals, two others, Doug Sherman and William Hendricks, found that Christians were almost as likely as unbelievers to do such things as steal from the workplace, falsify their income tax, and selectively obey laws.

To truly claim to be a Christian, a person must do far more than go to church occasionally. He or she must strive to be Christlike 24 hours a day, 365 days a year, in all situations and all circumstances.

*Don't work hard only when your master
is watching and then shirk when he isn't
looking; work hard and with gladness
all the time, as though working for Christ,
doing the will of God with all your hearts.*
EPHESIANS 6:6-7 TLB

> Don't ask God for what you think is good; ask Him for what He thinks is good for you.

During a prayer meeting one night, an elderly woman pleaded, "It really doesn't matter what You do with us, Lord; just have Your way with our lives." Adelaide Pollard, a rather well-known itinerant Bible teacher, overheard her prayer. At the time, she was deeply discouraged because she had been unable to raise the money she needed to go to Africa for missionary service. She was moved by this woman's sincere request of God, and when she went home that evening, she meditated on Jeremiah 18:3-4: "Then I went down to the potter's house, and behold, he wrought a work on the wheels, and the vessel that he made of clay was marred in the hand of the potter; so he made it again another vessel, as seemed good to the potter to make it." Before retiring, Adelaide took pen in hand and wrote in hymn form her own prayer:

Have Thine own way, Lord! Have Thine own way! Thou art the potter, I am the clay. Mold me and make me after Thy will, while I am waiting, yielded and still.

Have Thine own way, Lord! Have Thine own way! Search me, and try me, Master today! Whiter than snow, Lord, wash me just now, as in Thy presence humbly I bow.

After this manner therefore pray ye. . . .
Thy kingdom come. Thy will be
done in earth, as it is in heaven.
MATTHEW 6:9-10

Wally started baking chocolate chip cookies for his friends in 1970, using a recipe and procedure he had received from his Aunt Della. For five years, he gave away every batch he made, even though people often told him that his cookies were so good that he should go into business and sell them. Wally, however, had other ideas. He was intent on being a big-time show-business manager.

> Opportunities are seldom labeled.

Then one day a friend, B. J. Gilmore, said to him that she had a friend who could put up the money for a cookie-making business. Her friend never made the investment, but Wally got some of his friends—including Jeff Wall, Helen Reddy, and Marvin Gaye—to put up some money. And Wally was off and running.

Originally he intended to open up only one store on Sunset Boulevard, just enough to "make a living." After all, his was the only store in the world dedicated only to the sale of chocolate chip cookies. But business grew virtually overnight. Wally's "Famous Amos Chocolate Chip" cookies were soon distributed worldwide. Wally, himself, became a spokesman for other products, from eggs to airlines to a telephone company. While he once dreamed of managing "stars," he became one in his own right!

Seek, and ye shall find; knock, and it shall be opened unto you.
MATTHEW 7:7

> ## The wise does at once what the fool does at last.

An old legend recounts how Satan once called three of his top aides so that they might make a plan about how to stop the effective outreach of a particular group of Christians.

One of the aides, Rancor, proposed, "We should convince them there is no God." Satan sneered at Rancor and replied, "That would never work. They know there's a God."

Bitterness then spoke up, "We'll convince them that God does not really care about right and wrong." Satan thought about the idea for a few moments but then rejected it. "Too many know that God cares," he finally said.

Malice then proposed his idea. "We'll let them go on thinking there is a God and that He cares about right and wrong. But we will keep whispering that there is no hurry, there is no hurry, there is no hurry."

Satan howled with delight! The plan was adopted, and Malice was promoted to an even higher position in Satan's malevolent hierarchy.

Who can tell how many souls have been lost or lives sorely wounded because someone has held to the commonly acceptable notion: *Delay is OK.*

He that gathereth in summer is a wise son: but he that sleepeth in harvest is a son that causeth shame.
PROVERBS 10:5

After years of working in Rome on sculptures that were the "size of life," Michelangelo went to Florence, where a large block of splendid white Carrara marble had been obtained for a colossal statue. Within weeks, he had signed an agreement to complete a rendition of David for the cathedral. Contract in hand, he started in at once, working with furious energy so great that he often slept in his clothes, grudging the time it took to take them off and put them on again. He examined and measured the marble minutely to see what pose it could accommodate . . . made sketches of possible attitudes and careful, detailed drawings from models . . . tested his ideas in wax on a small scale. And only then did he pick up a point and mallet.

> Nothing great was ever achieved without enthusiasm.

Michelangelo approached painting the ceiling of the Sistine Chapel with the same energy. He took only a month to develop the theme, then launched with a fury into the final design, designing scaffolding, and hiring helpers. Lying at uncomfortable angles on hard boards, breathing the suffocating air just under the vault, plaster dust inflaming his eyes and irritating his skin, he spent much of the next four years literally sweating in physical distress as he worked.

He was an artist of *passionate* enthusiasm!

The joy of the Lord is your strength.
NEHEMIAH 8:10

Trust in yourself and you are doomed to disappointment; . . . but trust in God, and you are never to be confounded in time or eternity.

Marian had her sights set on becoming a concert singer, a challenge that was doubly difficult because of the color of her skin. Her mother, however, had a patient trust in God. Marian later said, "Mother's religion made her believe that she would receive what was right for her to have if she was conscientious in her faith. If it did not come, it was because He had not considered it right for her. We grew in this atmosphere of faith that she created. . . . We believed as she did because we wanted the same kind of haven in the time of storm."

When Marian was denied admission to a famous music conservatory on account of her race, her mother calmly said that "someone would be raised up" to help her accomplish what she had hoped to do at the conservatory. That someone arrived only a few weeks later. One of Philadelphia's outstanding voice teachers, Guiseppe Boghetti, made room for her to become one of his students, and Marian Anderson was on her way to becoming one of the most magnificent singers in the twentieth century. On Easter Sunday in 1939, she sang for more than 75,000 people gathered in front of the Lincoln Memorial and gave a performance never forgotten by those who were there.

It is better to take refuge in the
LORD than to trust in man.
PSALM 118:8 NIV

During the late 1960s, a couple was vacationing in the California mountains one day and they noticed a pleasant-appearing young man sitting by a bridge near their hotel. They saw him sitting in that same spot day after day. At first, they assumed he was fishing, but on closer look, they saw he was doing nothing—just sitting and staring into space. Finally, on the last day of their vacation, their curiosity came to a climax and they asked the young man, "Why do you sit in that one spot all day, every day?"

> Don't be discouraged; everyone who got where he is started where he was.

He replied with a smile, "I happen to believe in reincarnation. I believe that I have lived many times before and that I will have many lives following this one. So this life I'm sitting out."

In reality, it's impossible for any of us to "sit out" life. Each day, we are either moving forward or backward, getting stronger or weaker, moving higher or slipping lower. Each of us begins each new day with a fresh opportunity to change tomorrow's "starting point."

What will you do today to make your tomorrow better?

Though your beginning was insignificant,
Yet your end will increase greatly.
JOB 8:7 NASB

> **Maturity doesn't come with age; it comes with acceptance of responsibility.**

A number of definitions of maturity have been offered by experts, but these are perhaps among the best understood by the average person:

Maturity is not only wanting to have a puppy to call your own . . . but remembering on your own to give it fresh water and food every day.

Maturity is not only knowing how to dress yourself . . . but remembering to put your dirty clothes in the laundry hamper after you've taken them off.

Maturity is not only being capable of using a telephone to call a friend . . . but knowing how to keep your calls short so others can have access to the phone.

Maturity is not only being old enough to stay at home alone . . . but being able to be trusted to stay at home with only your friends.

Maturity is not only being old enough to drive the car by yourself . . . but paying for the gasoline you use.

Maturity is not only being old enough to stay up late . . . but being wise enough to go to bed early.

When I was a child, I spake as a child,
I understood as a child, I thought as
a child: but when I became a man,
I put away childish things.
1 CORINTHIANS 13:11

The difference between success and failure is often the ability to get up just one more time than you fall down!

Moses could have given up easily. He had an "interrupted" childhood, lived with a foster family, had a strong temper, a stammering tongue, and a criminal record; but when God called to him, he said "yes."

Joshua had seen the Promised Land and then been forced to wander in a wilderness for 40 years with cowards who didn't believe, as he did, that they could possess the land. He could have given up in discouragement, but he was willing to go when God said to go.

Peter had a hard time making the transition from fisherman to fisher of men. He sank

The man who wins may have been counted out several times, but he didn't hear the referee.

while trying to walk on water, was strongly rebuked by Jesus for trying to tell Him what to do, and denied knowing Jesus in the very hour Jesus needed him most. He could have seen himself to be a hopeless failure. But when the opportunity came to preach before thousands on the Day of Pentecost, he responded.

No matter what you've done, you're not a failure unless you give up.

*Though a righteous man falls
seven times, he rises again.*
PROVERBS 24:16 NIV

> The happiest people don't necessarily
> have the best of everything.
> They just make the best of everything.

A story is told of identical twins, one a hope-filled optimist who often said, "Everything is coming up roses!" The other twin was a sad and hopeless pessimist who continually expected the worst to happen. The concerned parents of the twins took them to a psychologist in hopes he might be able to help them balance their personalities.

The psychologist suggested that on the twins' next birthday the parents put them in separate rooms to open their gifts. "Give the pessimist the best toys you can afford," the psychologist said, "and give the optimist a box of manure." The parents did as he said.

When they peeked in on the pessimistic twin, they heard him audibly complaining, "I don't like the color of this toy . . . I'll bet this toy will break . . . I don't like to play this game . . . I know someone who has a bigger toy than this."

Tiptoeing across the corridor, the parents peeked in and saw their optimistic son gleefully throwing manure up in the air. He was giggling as he said, "You can't fool me! Where there's this much manure, there's gotta be a pony!"

How are you looking at life today? As an accident waiting to happen, or a blessing about to be received?

I have learned, in whatsoever state I am, therewith to be content. I can do all things through Christ which strengtheneth me.
PHILIPPIANS 4:11,13

A missionary surgeon in one of China's hospitals restored sight to a man who had been nearly blinded by cataracts. A few weeks later, to his great surprise, 48 blind men showed up on his hospital's doorstep. They had all come to be cured. Amazingly, these blind men had walked more than 250 miles from a remote area of China to get to the hospital. They had traveled by holding on to a rope chain. Their guide, and their inspiration, was the man who had been cured.

> Keep company with good men and good men you will imitate.

The Christian evangelist Dr. J. Wilbur Chapman concluded from his study of the New Testament Gospels that Jesus healed some forty people personally. Of this number, thirty-four were brought to Him or to His attention by friends of family members, or Jesus was taken to the ailing person by others. Only six of the forty people healed in the Gospels found their way to Jesus, or He to them, *without* someone assisting.

In the Gospels, Jesus refers to His followers as "friends." To them, He was the Friend of Friends, closer even than a brother. Not only do we become like friends with whom we associate, but when our friends are like Jesus, we find ourselves more likely to imitate Him!

Iron sharpeneth iron; so a man sharpeneth the countenance of his friend.
PROVERBS 27:17

> ## Learn by experience—
> ## preferably other people's.

Famous World War II general, George S. Patton, Jr., was an avid reader and student of history. He wrote to his son in 1944: "To be a successful soldier, you must know history. Read it objectively. . . . In Sicily I decided as a result of my information, observations, and a sixth sense that I have that the enemy did not have another large-scale attack in his system. I bet my shirt on that and I was right." His sixth sense may very well have been formed by thousands of hours of reading history, biographies, and autobiographies.

Historical parallels were constantly on Patton's mind. When he observed the situation in Normandy on July 2, 1944, he immediately wrote Eisenhower that the German Schlieffen

Plan of 1914 could be applied. A month later an operation such as he had described brought about the German defeat in Normandy.

Perhaps the book that influenced Patton most was Ardant du Picq's *Battle Studies*. Patton used it to help solve the problem of getting infantry to advance through enemy artillery fire. He recommended it to Eisenhower: "First read *Battle Studies* by du Picq (you can get a copy at Leavenworth); then put your mind to a solution." Are *you* interested in a particular field of study? Immerse yourself in its history.

All these things happened to them as examples—as object lessons to us—to warn us against doing some of the same things.
1 CORINTHIANS 10:11 TLB

The story is told of a foreman who went to check on the labor of several workers at a building site in medieval France. He approached the first worker and asked, "What are you doing?"

The man snapped back, "Are you blind? I'm cutting these impossible boulders with primitive tools and putting them together the way I've been told. I'm sweating under this blazing sun doing this backbreaking work, and it's boring me to death."

It is not what a man does that determines whether his work is sacred or secular; it is why he does it.

The foreman quickly backed off and retreated to a second worker, asking the same question. "What are you doing?" This worker replied matter-of-factly, "I'm shaping these boulders into usable forms, which are then assembled according to the architect's plans. It's hard work and sometimes it gets repetitive, but I earn five francs a week and that supports my wife and children. It's a job. Could be worse, could be better."

Feeling somewhat encouraged, the foreman went on to a third worker, asking, "What are you doing?" The worker lifted his eyes to the sky and said, "Why, can't you see? I'm building a cathedral for God!"

The meaning you give to your work or study today will directly impact the satisfaction you feel at the day's end.

Whatever you do, work at it
with all your heart, as working
for the Lord, not for men. . . .
It is the Lord Christ you are serving.
COLOSSIANS 3:23-24 NIV

> It's not hard to make decisions
> when you know what
> your values are.

Marshall Field once offered the following twelve reminders to help a person obtain a sound sense of values:

The value of time.
The success of perseverance.
The pleasure of working.
The dignity of simplicity.
The worth of character.
The power of kindness.
The influence of example.
The obligation of duty.
The wisdom of economy.
The virtue of patience.
The improvement of talent.
The joy of originating.

Can you state the core principles of your value system today? For some, it is likely to be the Ten Commandments. For others, the sayings of Jesus.

Solid values are like unmarred, evenly hewn stones. No matter what you build with them, you can be sure that if you follow the basic laws of construction the structure will be sound, resilient in storms, and long-lasting.

Daniel purposed in his heart that he would not defile himself.
DANIEL 1:8

Consider the "downside" of immorality when it is found out:

Your family experiences shame, rejection, betrayal, and heartache. No amount of repentance or asking forgiveness can soften the blow. Suspicion replaces trust.

The trust of your family is dealt a devastating blow.

You are likely to be embarrassed in facing other Christians, especially those who have openly appreciated, respected, and trusted you.

Conquer yourself rather than the world.

If you are engaged in the Lord's work, you will suffer great damage in your ministry and a dark shadow will accompany you everywhere. Forgiveness won't erase it.

Your fall may be perceived by others as license to do the same.

Your own inner peace will be gone.

Your enemies will have further reason to jeer and sneer at you.

What a high price to pay for failing to conquer one's own emotions and desires!

Similarly, encourage the young men to be self-controlled.
TITUS 2:6 NIV

> I am only one; but still I am one. I cannot
> do everything, but still I can do something;
> I will not refuse to do the something I can do.

Jewish physician Boris Kornfeld was imprisoned in Siberia. There, he worked in surgery, helping both the staff and prisoners. He met a Christian, whose name is unknown, but whose quiet faith and frequent reciting of the Lord's Prayer moved Dr. Kornfeld.

One day while repairing the slashed artery of a guard, Dr. Kornfeld seriously considered suturing the artery in such a way that the guard would bleed to death internally over time. The violence he recognized in his own heart appalled him, and he found himself saying, "Forgive us our sins as we forgive those who sin against us." Afterward, he began to refuse to obey various inhumane, immoral prison camp rules. He knew his quiet rebellion put his life in danger.

One afternoon he examined a patient who had undergone a cancer operation. He saw in the man's eyes a depth of spiritual misery that moved him, and he told him his entire story, including a confession of his secret faith. That very night, Dr. Kornfeld was murdered as he slept. Still, his testimony was not in vain. The patient who had heard his confession became, as a result, a Christian. He survived the prison camp and went on to tell the world about life in the gulag. That patient was Aleksandr Solzhenitsyn.

Under his [Christ's] direction the whole body is fitted together perfectly, and each part in its own special way helps the other parts.
EPHESIANS 4:16 TLB

In 1865, after General Ulysses Grant had moved his occupying army into Shiloh, he ordered a seven o'clock curfew for the city. One distinguished Southern lady, a Mrs. Johnson, was seen walking near the army's downtown headquarters near the curfew time.

General Grant approached her and said, "Mrs. Johnson, it's a little dangerous out there. I am going to ask two of my officers to escort you home."

She replied determinedly, "I won't go."

Grant smiled, went back into his headquarters, and returned in a few minutes wearing an overcoat that covered his insignia and rank.

"May I walk with you, Mrs. Johnson?" he asked.

> **Politeness goes far yet costs nothing.**

"Why, yes," Mrs. Johnson replied, nearly blushing. "I'm always glad to have a gentleman as an escort."

Mrs. Johnson would walk with a man she saw as a *gentleman,* even though she would not walk with a Union soldier. Good manners and genuine politeness go a long way toward "covering" many of our faults and mistakes.

A kind man benefits himself.
PROVERBS 11:17 NIV

> We should behave to our friends
> as we would wish our friends
> to behave to us.

Harry Truman had a reputation for never having been sly or disloyal in his life. He stood by a friend even when he risked public ridicule for it.

One of Truman's friends from his army days was Jim Pendergast, whose Uncle Tom was the head of the Democratic Party in Kansas City. Jim and his dad urged Truman to "run for office"—meaning a judgeship in rural Jackson County. A year later, Truman did so and, with Pendergast's support, won the election. As judge, he didn't always agree with Pendergast's practices. Tom once said to a group of contractors who had asked him to influence Truman: "I told you he was the hardheadest, orneriest man in the world; there isn't anything I can do."

Unfortunately, Pendergast's penchant for horse races caused him to be investigated for income tax evasion. He confessed, was fined, and was sentenced to serve fifteen months in a federal penitentiary. When Pendergast died during Truman's vice presidency, Truman didn't hesitate "for even five seconds" to fly to Kansas City for the funeral. "He was always my friend," Truman said of him, "and I have always been his."

True friendship is not based on what a friend does for you, but on what he means to you.

As ye would that men should do to you,
do ye also to them likewise.
LUKE 6:31

In 1947, Dr. Chandrasekhar was scheduled to teach an advanced seminar in astrophysics at the University of Chicago. At the time, he was living in Wisconsin, doing research at the Yerkes astronomical observatory. He faced an in-the-dead-of-winter, twice-a-week, 100-mile commute to teach the class, but he nonetheless agreed enthusiastically.

Registration for the advanced seminar, however, fell far below expectations. In fact, only two students signed up for the class. Other faculty members expected Dr. Chandrasekhar to cancel the course so as not to waste his valuable time. He determined, however, to continue with the course and give his very best to the two students registered.

> The end must justify the means.

Those students, Chen Ning Yang and Tsung-Dao Lee, made his effort worthwhile. Ten years later, in 1957, they both won the Nobel prize for physics. Dr. Chandrasekhar later won that same award in 1983.

Ends and means are not meant to exist in conflict. *Good* means to *good* ends are what God challenges us to find and to do, regardless of the personal cost, the effort required, or a lack of public acclaim. *The best pursuit of the best ideals* is what makes for integrity.

The just man walketh in his integrity:
his children are blessed after him.
PROVERBS 20:7

Character is what you are in the dark.

Have you ever watched an icicle form? Did you notice how the dripping water froze, one drop at a time, until the icicle was a foot long, or more?

If the water was clean, the icicle remained clear and sparkled brightly in the sun; but if the water was slightly muddy, the icicle looked cloudy, its beauty spoiled.

In just this manner our character is formed. Each thought or feeling adds its influence. Each decision we make—about matters both great and small—contributes. Every bit that we take into our minds and souls—be they impressions, experiences, visual images, or the words of others—help create our character.

We must remain concerned at all times about the "droplets" that we allow to drip through our lives. Acts that develop habits of love, truth, and goodness silently mold and fashion us into the image of God—just as habits born of hate, falsehood, and evil intent mar and eventually destroy us.

The integrity of the upright shall guide them.
PROVERBS 11:3

As a senior in high school, Jim batted .427 and led his team in home runs. He also quarter-backed his football team to the state semifinals. Jim later went on to pitch professionally for the New York Yankees.

That's a remarkable achievement for any athlete. But it's an almost unbelievable one for Jim, who was born without a right hand.

A little boy who had only parts of two fingers on one of his hands once came to Jim in the club-house after a Yankees game and said, "They call me crab at camp. Did kids ever tease you?"

Adversity causes some men to break, others to break records.

"Yeah," Jim replied. "Kids used to tell me that my hand looked like a foot." And then he asked the boy an all-important question. "Is there anything you can't do?" The boy answered, "No."

"Well, I don't think so either," Jim responded.

What others see as your "limitation" today is only a limitation if *you* think it is. God certainly doesn't see you as limited. He sees you as having unlimited potential. When we begin to see ourselves the way God sees us, there truly are no limits to what we can do!

If thou faint in the day of adversity, thy strength is small.
PROVERBS 24:10

To love what you do and feel that it matters—how could anything be more fun?

An English newspaper once posed this question to its readers: "Who are the happiest people on earth?" These were selected as the four prize-winning answers:

A craftsman or artist whistling over a job well done.

A little child building sand castles.

A mother, after a busy day, bathing her baby.

A doctor who has finished a difficult and dangerous operation and saved a human life.

Notice that none of these four were millionaires, leaders of nations, or those who have achieved high rank. True fun in life is found in the course of normal daily events that give a sense of accomplishment and meaning. As

W. Beran Wolfe once said, "If you observe a really happy man you will find him building a boat, writing a symphony, educating his son, growing double dahlias in his garden, or looking for dinosaur eggs on the Gobi desert. He will not be searching for happiness as if it were a collar button that has rolled under the radiator. He will not be striving for it as a goal in itself. He will have become aware that he is happy in the course of living life twenty-four crowded hours of the day."

My heart rejoiced in all my labour.
ECCLESIASTES 2:10

In 1643, a young shoemaker's apprentice went to Leicestershire, England, for a business fair. While there, he was invited by a cousin and another friend to share a jug of beer with them in the pub where they had gone to eat. Being thirsty, he joined them.

After each of the men had drunk a glass apiece, the man's cousin and friend began to drink to the health of first this one and then the other. They agreed that the person who didn't join in with their toasts would have to pay for the jug. This shocked the serious shoemaker's apprentice.

> A man who wants to lead the orchestra must turn his back on the crowd.

He rose from the table, took out a coin, and said simply, "If it be so, I will leave you.

At that, he left the pub and spent much of the night walking up and down the streets of the city, praying and crying to the Lord. The Lord spoke to him these words as recorded in his journal: "Thou seest how young people go together into vanity and old people into the earth. Thou must forsake all—young and old—keep out of all, and be as a stranger unto all." In obedience to this command, the young man left his relatives and his house and became a wonderer in England. His name? George Fox, the founder of the Quakers.

Wherefore come out from among them, and be ye separate, saith the Lord, and touch not the unclean thing; and I will receive you.

2 CORINTHIANS 6:17

> # Men are alike in their promises.
> # It is only in their deeds
> # that they differ.

When Teddy Roosevelt was asked to give a speech to the Naval War College in Newport, Rhode Island, on June 2, 1897, readiness was his theme. He insisted the only way to keep peace was to be ready for war, and the only way to be ready for war was to enlarge the Navy. It was a rousing, patriotic speech. The following February, the *Maine* was blown up, killing 264 sailors, and Americans across the land cried, "Remember the *Maine!*" In April, President McKinley asked Congress to declare war.

Not surprised that he backed the war effort, most Americans *were* surprised when Teddy Roosevelt resigned from his position as assistant secretary of the Navy three weeks after the war declaration . . . so that he'd be ready to fight. His friends told him he was crazy for throwing away his political future. His wife was against it. Yet all who knew Roosevelt well knew, even as they made them, that their protests were in vain. He had to join the effort. He later wrote that he wanted to be able to tell his children why he *had* fought in the war, not why he *hadn't* fought in it. As far as he was concerned, a person simply couldn't preach one thing and then do another.

Many a man claims to have unfailing love,
but a faithful man who can find?
PROVERBS 20:6 NIV

During the four-week siege of Tientsin, during the June 1900 Boxer Rebellion, Herbert Hoover helped erect barricades around the foreign compound and organized all the able-bodied men into a protective force to man them. Mrs. Hoover went to work, too—helping set up a hospital, taking her turn nursing the wounded, rationing food, and serving tea every afternoon to those on sentry duty. Like her husband, she remained calm and efficient throughout the crisis and even seemed to enjoy the excitement.

> Don't cross your bridges until you get to them. We spend our lives defeating ourselves crossing bridges we never get to.

One afternoon, while sitting at home playing solitaire to rest after her work at the hospital, a shell suddenly burst nearby. She ran to the back door and found a big hole in the backyard. A little later a second shell hit the road in front of the house. Then came a third shell. This one burst through one of the windows of the house and demolished a post by the staircase.

Several reporters covering the siege rushed into the living room to see if she was all right and found her at the card table. "I don't seem to be winning this hand," she remarked coolly, "but that was the third shell and therefore the last one for the present anyway. Their pattern is three in a row." Then she suggested brightly, "Let's go and have tea."

Don't be anxious about tomorrow.
God will take care of your tomorrow
too. Live one day at a time.
MATTHEW 6:34 TLB

> # He that has learned to obey will know how to command.

The story is told of a great military captain, who after a full day of battle, sat by a warming fire with several of his officers and began talking over the events of the day with them.

He asked them, "Who did the best today on the field of battle?"

One officer told of a man who had fought very bravely all day, and then just before dusk, had been severely wounded. Another told of a man who had taken a hit for a fellow soldier, sparing his friend's life but very possibly losing his own. Yet another told of the man who had led the charge into battle. And still another told of a soldier who had risked his life to pull a fellow soldier into a trench.

The captain heard them out and then said, "No, I fear you are all mistaken. The best man in the field today was the soldier who was just lifting up his arm to strike the enemy, but, upon hearing the trumpet sound the retreat, checked himself, dropped his arm without striking the blow, and retreated. That perfect and ready obedience to the will of his general is the noblest thing that was done today on the battlefield."

The wise in heart accept commands,
but a chattering fool comes to ruin.
PROVERBS 10:8 NIV

In 1877, George Eastman dreamed that the wonderful world of photography might be accessible to the average person. At the time, photographers working outdoors had to carry several items of bulky equipment and a corrosive agent called silver nitrate. Eastman realized that if he could eliminate much of this equipment, he would have something. Working in a bank by day, he spent his nights reading books on chemistry and magazines about photography. He took foreign language lessons so he could read information published in

> You must have long-range goals to keep you from being frustrated by short-range failures.

France and Germany. And then, with a partner, he began his own company in 1881. Almost immediately, a problem arose with the new "dry plates" he had invented. Eastman refunded the money to those who had purchased them and retired to his lab. Three months and 472 experiments later, he came up with the durable emulsion he was looking for!

Eastman spent many nights sleeping in a hammock at his factory after long days designing equipment. To replace the glass used for photographic plates, he created a roll of thin, flexible material now known as film. To replace heavy tripods, he developed a pocket camera. By 1895, photography was at last available for the "common man."

Keep your eyes on Jesus, our leader and instructor. He was willing to die a shameful death on the cross because of the joy he knew would be his afterwards; and now he sits in the place of honor by the throne of God.

HEBREWS 12:2 TLB

Clear your mind
of can't.

Harry Houdini, who won fame as an escape artist early in the twentieth century, issued a challenge wherever he went. He claimed he could be locked in any jail cell in the country and set himself free within minutes. He had a long track record of doing just that!

One time, however, something seemed to go wrong. Houdini entered a jail cell in his street clothes. The heavy metal doors clanged shut behind him, and he took from his belt a concealed piece of strong and flexible metal. He set to work on the lock to his cell, but something seemed different about this particular lock. For thirty minutes he worked without results. An hour passed. This was long after the time that Houdini normally freed himself and he began to sweat and pant in exasperation. Still, he could not pick the lock.

Finally, after laboring for two hours, Houdini—feeling a sense of failure close in around him—leaned in frustration against the door he could not unlock. To his amazement, as he collapsed against the door, it swung open! *It had not been locked in the first place!*

How many times are challenges impossible—or doors locked—only because we *think* they are? When we put our minds and energy toward them, we often find the impossible tasks turned into achievements.

> *I can do all things through Christ*
> *which strengtheneth me.*
> PHILIPPIANS 4:13

Grace Hopper seemed to be born with a desire to discover how things worked. At age seven, her curiosity led her to dismantle every clock in her childhood home! She eventually completed a doctorate in mathematics from Yale. During World War II, Grace joined the Navy and was assigned to the Navy's computation project at Harvard University. She met "Harvard Mark I," the first fully functional digital computing machine. Once again, Grace set about to learn how its 750,000 parts and 500 miles of wire worked! While most experts believed computers were too complicated and expensive for anyone but highly trained scientists to use, Grace had her own idea: make them easier to operate so more people could use

The future belongs to those who believe in the beauty of their dreams.

them. Her work gave rise to the programming language COBOL.

As late as 1963, each large computer had its own master language. Grace became an advocate for universally accepted systems. She envisioned a day when computers would one day be small enough to sit on a desk, be more powerful than Harvard Mark I, and be useful in offices, schools, and at home. With rank of rear admiral, she retired from the Navy at age 80. More important to her, she had lived to see her dream of personal computers come true!

"Anything is possible if you have faith."
MARK 9:23 TLB

The future belongs to those
who see possibilities before
they become obvious.

ENIAC was one of the first computers to use electronic circuits, which made for lightning-fast calculations. Former chairman of IBM, Thomas J. Watson, Jr., at first saw no use for it. He said, "I reacted to ENIAC the way some people probably reacted to the Wright brothers' airplane. It didn't move me at all. . . . I couldn't see this gigantic, costly, unreliable device as a piece of business equipment."

A few weeks later, he and his friends wandered into a research office at IBM and saw an engineer with a high-speed punch-card machine hooked up to a black box. When asked what he was doing, he said, "Multiplying with radio tubes." The machine was tabulating a payroll at one-tenth the time it took the standard punch-card machine to do so. Watson recalls, "That impressed me as though somebody had hit me on the head with a hammer." He said, "Dad, we should put this thing on the market! Even if we only sell eight or ten, we'll be able to advertise the fact that we have the world's first commercial electronic calculator."

And that's how IBM got into electronics. Within a year, IBM had electronic circuits that both multiplied and divided, and at that point, electronic calculators became truly useful. Thousands of the IBM 604 were sold.

The vision is yet for an appointed time . . .
it will surely come, it will not tarry.
HABAKKUK 2:3

When Michigan played Wisconsin in basketball early in the 1989 season, Michigan's Rumeal Robinson found himself at the foul line with just seconds left in the fourth quarter. His team was trailing by one point, and Rumeal knew that if he could sink both shots, Michigan would win. Sadly, Rumeal missed both shots. Wisconsin upset the favored Michigan, and Rumeal went to the locker room feeling devastated and embarrassed.

> When I was a young man I observed that nine out of ten things I did were failures. I didn't want to be a failure, so I did ten times more work.

His dejection, however, led to a positive move on his part. He determined that at the end of each practice for the rest of the season, he was going to shoot 100 extra foul shots. And shoot 'em he did!

The moment came when Rumeal stepped to the foul line in yet another game, again with the opportunity to make two shots. This time there were only three seconds left in overtime, and the game was the NCAA finals! Swish went the first shot . . . and swish went the second. Those two points gave Michigan the victory and the collegiate national championship for the season.

Have you just failed at something? Don't give up. Instead, work harder. Success is possible!

He becometh poor that dealeth with
a slack hand: but the hand
of the diligent maketh rich.
PROVERBS 10:4

> ## Luck is a matter of preparation
> ## meeting opportunity.

We can learn a great deal from the Alaskan bull moose. Each fall, during the breeding season, the males of the species battle for dominance. They literally go head-to-head, antlers crunching together as they collide. When antlers are broken, defeat is ensured since a moose's antlers are its only weapon.

Generally speaking, the heftiest moose with the largest and strongest antlers wins. Therefore, the battle is nearly always predetermined the summer before. It is then that the moose eat nearly round the clock. The one that consumes the best diet for growing antlers and gaining weight will be the victor. Those who eat inadequately will have weaker antlers and less bulk. The fight itself involves far more brawn than brain, with more reliance on bulk than on skill.

The lesson for us? Spiritual battles are inevitable. We each experience "seasons of attack" in our lives. Whether we are victorious or fall victim depends not on our skills or brainpower, but on our spiritual strength. What we do in advance of the war determines the outcome of the battle. Now is the time to develop enduring faith, strength, and wisdom. Now is the time for prayer, reading and memorizing God's Word, and hearing the Gospel preached!

Make the most of every opportunity.
COLOSSIANS 4:5 NIV

Most communication researchers and theorists contend that the first step in effective communication is "gaining attention." In order to establish lines of communication, you must "attend" to them—really see, hear, listen, and feel what they feel.

The Hebrew word for "attend" has several meanings. Two of them paint vivid descriptions about the listening process:

> Jumping to conclusions is not half as good an exercise as digging for facts.

A sharpened ear. Such ears are like those of an animal listening to an unusual sound. Imagine a dog's ears "perked up" to listen. Listen to those speaking to you with a heightened awareness.

A bent ear. This is the ear that is "cocked" in a certain direction—the ear positioned so that it hears fully and clearly, without distortion. Get rid of distractions and focus on the person speaking to you.

Listening takes effort. It can be far more draining than talking but it is key in communication.

Study to shew thyself approved unto God,
a workman that needeth not to be ashamed,
rightly dividing the word of truth.
2 TIMOTHY 2:15

> The most valuable of all talents
> is that of never using
> two words when one will do.

Albert Einstein is reputed to have had a wholesome disregard for the tyranny of custom. Once, a dinner, hosted by the president of Swarthmore College, was held in his honor. Although Einstein was not scheduled to speak during the event—only to receive an award—after the award was made, the audience clamored "Speech, speech." The president turned the podium over to him. Einstein reluctantly came forward and said only this: "Ladies and gentlemen, I am very sorry but I have nothing to say." And then he sat down.

A few seconds later he stood back up and said, "In case I do have something to say, I'll come back."

Some six months later, Einstein wired the president of the college with this message: "Now I have something to say."

Another dinner was held, and this time, Einstein made a speech.

If you have nothing to say, it's wise to say nothing. If you have something to say, it's wise to say it in as few words as possible. As the old saying goes, "If your mind should go blank, don't forget to turn off the sound."

In the multitude of words there wanteth not sin: but he that refraineth his lips is wise.
PROVERBS 10:19

Henry Ward Beecher, one of the most powerful preachers in American history, gave this illustration in one of his sermons:

The lobster, when left high and dry among the rocks, has no sense or energy enough to work his way back to the sea but waits for the sea to come to him. If it does not come, he remains where he is and dies, although the slightest exertion would enable him to reach the waves, which are perhaps tossing and tumbling within a yard of him.

Laziness is often mistaken for patience.

There is a tide in human affairs that casts men into "tight places" and leaves them there, like stranded lobsters. If they choose to lie where the breakers have flung them, expecting some grand billow to take them on its big shoulders and carry them to smooth water, the chances are that their hopes will never be realized.

Patience—so often associated with generosity and a long-suffering nature toward others, or a steadfast faith in God—is a virtue. It was never intended, however, to be an excuse for not exerting effort or not giving.

Let us lay aside every weight, and the sin which doth so easily beset us, and let us run with patience the race that is set before us.
HEBREWS 12:1

> One-half the trouble of this life can
> be traced to saying yes too quickly,
> and not saying no soon enough.

A man who had been quite successful in the manufacturing business decided to retire. He called in his son to tell him of his decision, saying, "Son, it's all yours as of the first of next month." The son, while eager to take over the firm and exert his own brand of leadership, also realized what a big responsibility he was facing. "I'd be grateful for any words of advice you have to give me," he said to his father.

The father advised, "Well, I've made a success of this business because of two principles: reliability and wisdom. First, take reliability. If you promise goods by the tenth of the month, no matter what happens, you must deliver by the tenth. Your customers won't understand any delay. They'll see a delay as failure. So, even if it costs you overtime, double time, golden time, you must deliver your promise."

The son mulled this over for a few moments and then asked, "And wisdom?" The father shot back: "Wisdom is never making such a stupid promise in the first place."

Be sure you can back up your words with evidence and deliver on your promises before you make them. A large part of your reputation depends on your ability to keep your word.

Seest thou a man that is hasty in his words? there is more hope of a fool than of him.
PROVERBS 29:20

When Honorius was emperor of Rome, the great Coliseum was often filled to overflowing with spectators who came from near and far to watch the state-sponsored games. Part of the sport venue consisted of human beings doing battle with wild beasts or one another—a battle to the death. The assembled multitudes made holiday of such sport and found the greatest delight when a human being died.

> I would rather fail in the cause that someday will triumph than triumph in a cause that someday will fail.

On just such a day, a Syrian monk named Telemachus was part of the vast crowd in the arena. Telemachus was cut to the core of his heart by the utter disregard he saw for the value of human life. He leaped from the spectator stands into the area during a gladiatorial show and cried out, "This thing is not right! This thing must stop!"

Because he had interfered, the authorities commanded that Telemachus be run through with a sword, which was done. He died, but not in vain. His cry kindled a small flame in the nearly burned-out conscience of the people and within a matter of months the gladiatorial combats came to an end.

The greater the wrong, the louder we must cry out against it. The finer the cause, the louder we must applaud!

Now thanks be unto God, which always causeth us to triumph in Christ.
2 CORINTHIANS 2:14

> ## Carve your name on hearts
> ## and not on marble.

When Salvation Army officer Shaw saw the three men before him, tears sprang to his eyes. Shaw was a medical missionary who had just arrived in India. The Salvation Army was taking over the leper colony where he had been assigned. The three men before him had manacles and fetters binding their hands and feet, cutting into their diseased flesh. Captain Shaw turned to the guard and said, "Please unfasten the chains."

"It isn't safe," the guard protested. "These men are dangerous criminals as well as lepers!"

"I'll be responsible," Captain Shaw said. "They are suffering enough." He then reached out, took the keys, knelt, tenderly removed the shackles from the men, and treated their bleeding ankles and wrists.

About two weeks later, Shaw had to make an overnight trip. He dreaded leaving his wife and child alone. The words of the guard came back to him regarding the safety of his family. When Shaw's wife went to the front door the morning she was alone, she was startled to see the three criminals lying on her steps. One of them explained, "We know the doctor go. We stay here all night so no harm come to you."

You never know how someone will respond to an act of love!

The only letter I need is you yourselves!. . .
They can see that you are a letter from
Christ written by us. . . . not one carved
on stone, but in human hearts.
2 CORINTHIANS 3:2-3 TLB

The Bible—carefully read and well-worn—was the most important book in Gerrit's house. His home was a house of prayer, where many tears were shed for revival in his church in Heemstede. Almost a generation later, his prayers were answered as that very church became the center of an upsurge of faith in Holland, part of the Great Awakening in Europe.

When she was about eighteen years old, Gerrit's great-granddaughter had a dream about him. He was walking through a beautiful park with her and he said, "When you sow some seed and put it in the ground, this seed will make a plant, and this plant will give seed again. . . . You, my dear Corrie, are the daughter of my grandson. . . . You are a plant, blooming from my seed. I will show you

> A knowledge of the Bible without a college course is more valuable than a college course without the Bible.

something that will never be changed. It is the Word of God." In the dream, he opened his Bible and said, "This Book will be the same forever." He then told her, "Plant the seeds from God's Book, and they will grow from generation to generation."

Corrie ten Boom did just that. She planted God's Word in hearts and minds around the world. Information learned in textbooks is continually updated. Courses of study change. The truths of the Bible, however, are absolutes. Its promises are sure.

All scripture is given by inspiration of God,
and is profitable for doctrine, for reproof, for
correction, for instruction in righteousness:
That the man of God may be perfect,
thoroughly furnished unto all good works.
2 TIMOTHY 3:16-17

> Little minds are tamed and
> subdued by misfortunes; but
> great minds rise above them.

When Aaron was eight months old, he stopped gaining weight. A few months later, his hair began to fall out. At first, doctors told Aaron's parents that he would be short as an adult, but otherwise be normal. Later, a pediatrician diagnosed the problem: progeria, or "rapid aging." Just as the pediatrician predicted, Aaron never grew beyond three feet in height, had no hair on his head or body, looked like an old man while still a child, and died of old age in his early teens. His father, a rabbi, felt a deep, aching sense of unfairness.

About a year and a half after Aaron's death, the father came to realize that none of us is ever promised a life free of pain or disappointment. Rather, the most any of us has been promised is that we need not be alone in our pain and that we can draw upon a source outside ourselves for strength and courage. He came to the conclusion that God does not cause our misfortunes, but rather, helps us by inspiring others to help.

Out of Harold Kushner's experience came a book that has helped millions, *When Bad Things Happen to Good People*. He says, "I think of Aaron and all that his life taught me, and I realize how much I have lost and how much I have gained. Yesterday seems less painful, and I am not afraid of tomorrow."

A just man falleth seven times,
and riseth up again.
PROVERBS 24:16

A very successful businessman was once interviewed by a young reporter. The reporter asked the man to give him a detailed history of his company. As the man talked at length, the reporter began to be amazed at the size and magnitude of the many problems the man had overcome. He finally asked him, "But how did you overcome so many problems of such great magnitude?"

The old gentleman leaned back in his chair and said, "There's really no trick to it." And then he added, "You know . . . there are some troubles that seem so high you can't climb over them." The reporter nodded in agreement, thinking of several he was currently facing. "And," the wise businessman went on, "there are some troubles so wide you can't walk around them."

> There is no poverty that can overtake diligence.

Again, the reporter nodded. The man went on, raising his voice dramatically, "And there are some problems too deep you can't dig under them." Eager for a solution, the reporter said, "Yes? Yes?"

"It's then," the man concluded, "that you know the only way to beat the problem is to duck your head and wade right through it."

A problem rarely decreases in size while a person stands and stares at it!

He becometh poor that dealeth
with a slack hand: but the
hand of the diligent maketh rich.
PROVERBS 10:4

> # Never despair; but if you do,
> # work on in despair.

American sports fans watched in awe on Sunday, March 4, 1979, as Phil took to the giant-slalom slopes at Whiteface Mountain, New York. He exploded onto the course and then settled into a powerful carving of the mountainside. At gate 35, tragedy struck. Phil hooked his inside ski on a pole, went flying head over heels, and crashed in a crumpled heap. The ski team physician described the injury as "the ultimate broken ankle"—a break of both the ankle and lower leg. He literally put the bones back together with a three-inch metal plate and seven screws.

The question was not whether Phil would ever ski again, but if he would *walk* again. Looking back, Phil describes the months after his injury as a time of deep despair. Still, he never entertained doubts about walking or skiing.

After two months on crutches and a highly self-disciplined exercise program, he forced himself to walk without limping. In August, he began skiing gentle slopes. Less than six months after the accident he entered a race in Australia and finished second. In February 1980, less than a year after his agonizing injury, Phil Mahre took on the same mountain where he had fallen . . . and won an Olympic silver medal.

As for you, be strong and do not give up,
for your work will be rewarded.
2 CHRONICLES 15:7 NIV

The Lord appeared to a man named Ananias in a vision and asked him to undertake what Ananias must surely have perceived as a dangerous mission: to go to the house of a man named Judas, lay his hands on a man named Saul of Tarsus, and pray that he might receive his sight. Saul had become blind while traveling to Damascus to persecute the Christians there, having the full intent of taking them captive to Jerusalem for trial, torture, and death. Even so, Ananias did as he was asked by the Lord, and within the hour, Saul's sight was restored.

> You can accomplish more in one hour with God than one lifetime without Him.

According to Christian legend, Ananias was a simple cobbler who had no idea what happened to Saul after that day, or how he had changed the course of human history by obeying God in a simple act that was part of Saul's transformation into the Apostle Paul. As he lay on his deathbed, Ananias looked up toward heaven and whispered, "I haven't done much, Lord. A few shoes sewn, a few sandals stitched. But what more could be expected of a poor cobbler?"

The Lord spoke in Ananias's heart, "Don't worry, Ananias, about how much you have accomplished—or how little. You were there in the hour I needed you to be there. And that is all that matters."

"With God all things are possible."
Matthew 19:26

If you don't stand for something you'll fall for anything!

Former President Harry S. Truman once remarked that no president of our nation has ever escaped abuse and even libel from the press. He noted that it was far more common than rare to find a president publicly called a traitor. Truman further concluded that the president who had not fought with Congress or the Supreme Court hadn't done his job.

What is true for an American President is also true for everyone else. No matter how small a person's job may be—no matter how low he may be on a particular organizational chart or strata of society—there will be those who oppose him, rebuke him, and perhaps even challenge him to a fight. That is why no person can expect to conduct himself as if he were trying to win a popularity contest. Rather, a person needs to chart the course he feels compelled to walk in life, and then to do so with head held high and his convictions intact. It's simply a matter of taking life in stride to recognize that every person will eventually face the test of ridicule and criticism as he upholds his principles or defends his morals.

No, being hit isn't abnormal. But collapsing from fear of a hit isn't inevitable. Stand firm in and for your faith and the Lord will stand with you!

"If you do not stand firm in your faith, you will not stand at all."

Isaiah 7:9 NIV

Country-music star Randy Travis and his wife, Lib, remember the lean days of his career—all 3,650 of them. For ten years, Lib did whatever it took to keep her club open long enough for somebody to discover Travis' talent. For his part, Randy sang his heart out, and when he wasn't singing, he fried catfish or washed dishes in the kitchen. Then it happened. Everything seemed to click for him. He had a hit called "On the Other Hand," an album contract, a tour offer, and a movie deal. He was hot! Everyone seemed to be calling him an overnight success.

> The difference between ordinary and extraordinary is that little extra effort.

Travis notes, "We were turned down more than once by every label in Nashville. But I'm kind of one to believe that if you work at something long enough and keep believing, sooner or later it will happen."

In many instances in life, it's extra effort that makes the difference. Money can buy a house . . . but loving touches turn it into a home. A sack lunch becomes a gourmet meal with a love note tucked into it. A meal is just food . . . but with candles and flowers, it's an occasion. Do *more* than is required of you today. Give the extra that makes life truly extraordinary.

Whatsoever thy hand findeth to do,
do it with thy might.
ECCLESIASTES 9:10

> # Man cannot discover new oceans unless he has the courage to lose sight of the shore.

Two baseball coaches were commiserating about the difficulty of recruiting quality players for their teams. Said one coach, "If only I could find a man who plays every position perfectly, always gets a hit and never strikes out, and never makes a fielding error." The other coach sighed in agreement and added, "Yeah, if we could just get him to lay down his hot dog and come down out of the stands."

Playing life's game to the fullest requires taking a risk. Without risk, life has little emotion, and little that can be counted as exhilaration or fulfillment.

To laugh is to risk appearing the fool.

To weep is to risk appearing sentimental.

To reach out for another is to risk involvement.

To expose feelings is to risk exposing one's true self.

To place ideas and dreams before a crowd is to risk ridicule.

To love is to risk not being loved in return.

To live is to risk dying.

To hope is to risk despair.

To try is to risk failure.

And yet, the person who risks nothing—does nothing, has nothing, and ultimately becomes nothing.

Peter got out of the boat, and walked on the water and came toward Jesus.

MATTHEW 14:29 NASB

In the 1920s, an English adventurer named Mallory led an expedition to try to conquer Mt. Everest. His first expedition failed. So did the second. Mallory made a third assault with a highly skilled and experienced team, but in spite of careful planning and extensive safety measures, an avalanche wiped out Mallory and most of his party. Upon their return to England, the few who had survived held a banquet to salute Mallory and those who had perished on the mountain. As the leader of the survivors stood to speak, he looked around the hall

> Every man is enthusiastic at times. One man has enthusiasm for thirty minutes, another has it for thirty days—but it is the man that has it for thirty years who makes a success in life.

at the framed pictures of Mallory and the others who had died. Then he turned his back to the crowd and faced a large picture of Mount Everest, which stood looming behind the banquet table like a silent, unbeatable giant.

With tears streaming down his face, he spoke to the mountain on behalf of his dead friends: "I speak to you, Mt. Everest, in the name of all brave men living, and those yet unborn. Mt. Everest, you defeated us once; you defeated us twice; you defeated us three times. But, Mt. Everest, we shall someday defeat you, because you can't get any bigger and we can."

Keep your enthusiasm. Keep persevering. Run *your* race until you cross the finish line!

Let us run with perseverance
the race marked out for us.
HEBREWS 12:1 NIV

> Perseverance is a great element of success;
> if you only knock long enough and loud enough
> at the gate you are sure to wake up somebody.

We all know the power of gravity. The dropped hammer hits our toes rather than floats upward. We fall down, not up. But what many of us don't realize is that the gravitational *energy* of the whole earth has been estimated to amount only to a millionth of a horsepower! A toy magnet in the hands of a child probably has thousands of times more "energy."

What gravity lacks in energy, however, it makes up in tenacity. Gravity simply refuses to let go.

Not only is gravity tenacious, but it has far-reaching effects. Gravitational pull appears to be virtually limitless, reaching across the universe with nearly unimaginable power. Gravitational pull is what keeps the moon orbiting the earth, the planets revolving around the sun, and the sun, along with a billion other stars, rotating around the center of our galaxy like a cosmic pinwheel.

You may not have a great deal of power or energy today, but as the popular phrase states, you can "hang in there."

Don't stop believing with your faith!
Don't give up hope!
Don't let your love come to an end!

"Ask, and it shall be given you; seek, and ye shall find; knock, and it shall be opened unto you."
LUKE 11:9

In March 1987, Eamon Coughlan was running in a qualifying heat at the World Indoor Track Championships in Indianapolis. The Irishman was the reigning world record holder at 1500 meters and he was favored to win the race handily. Unfortunately, with two-and-a-half laps left to run, he was tripped and fell hard. Even so, he got up and, with great effort, he managed to catch the race leaders. With only twenty yards to go, he was in third place—which would have been good enough to qualify for the final race.

> Consider the postage stamp: its usefulness consists in the ability to stick to one thing till it gets there.

Then . . . Coughlan looked over his shoulder to the inside. Seeing no one there, he relaxed his effort slightly. What he hadn't noticed, however, was that a runner was charging hard on the outside. This runner passed Coughlan just a yard before the finish line, thus eliminating him from the finals. Coughlan's great comeback effort ended up being worthless for one and only one reason—he momentarily took his eyes off the finish line and focused on would-be competitors instead.

One of the most important factors in your reaching your goals in life is to have single-minded focus. Don't let yourself become distracted by what others do or say. Run *your* race to win!

I have fought a good fight, I have finished
my course, I have kept the faith.
2 TIMOTHY 4:7

> ## It needs more skill than I can tell
> ## to play the second fiddle well.

People often think of heart surgeons as being arrogant prima donnas in the medical world. But those who know Dr. William DeVries, the surgeon who pioneered the artificial heart, couldn't *disagree* more. Co-workers at Humana Hospital Audubon in Louisville, Kentucky, describe DeVries as the kind of doctor who shows up on Sundays to cheer discouraged patients. He occasionally changes dressings, traditionally considered a nurse's job, if a patient wants him to stick around and talk.

Friends say DeVries is an "old shoe" who fits in wherever he goes. He likes to wear cowboy boots with his surgical scrubs and he often repairs hearts to the beat of Vivaldi or jazz. "He has always got a smile lurking," says Louisville cardiologist Dr. Robert Goodin. "And he's always looking for a way to let it out."

No matter how high you rise, never forget that you started out at ground zero. Even if you were born to great wealth or privilege, you still were born as a helpless babe. Real success comes not in thinking you have arrived at a place where others should serve you, but in recognizing that in whatever place you are, you are in a position to serve others.

"He that is greatest among you shall be your servant."

MATTHEW 23:11

After several months of romance, Napoleon and Josephine decided to marry. The notary, who made out the marriage contract, was one of Josephine's friends. He secretly advised her against marrying "an obscure little officer who has nothing besides his uniform and sword and has no future." He thought she should find someone of greater worth. With her charms, he advised, she might attract a wealthy man, perhaps an army contractor or a business investor.

> A man never discloses his own character so clearly as when he describes another's.

Napoleon was in the next room while the notary was giving this advice to his beloved. He could hear every word he said. Still, he did not disclose that he had overheard.

After his coronation as Emperor, this very same notary appeared before him as a matter of business. At the conclusion of their appointment, Napoleon smiled and observed that Madame de Beauharnais—now that she was Queen of France—had done very well, after all, to have married that "obscure little officer who possessed nothing besides his uniform and sword and had no future."

The notary was forced to agree that she, indeed, had done well. As for himself—he was still a notary.

"A good man out of the good treasure of the heart bringeth forth good things: and an evil man out of the evil treasure bringeth forth evil things."
MATTHEW 12:35

The greatest use of life is to spend it for something that will outlast it.

Although we do not have the original manuscripts of the New Testament, we do have more than 99.9 percent of the original text because of the faithful work of manuscript copyists over the centuries.

Copying was a long, arduous process. In ancient days, copyists did not sit at desks while writing—but rather, stood or made copies while sitting on benches or stools, holding a scroll on their knees. Notes at the end of some scrolls tell of the drudgery of the work.

"He who does not know how to write supposes it to be no labor; but though only three fingers write, the whole body labors."

"Writing bows one's back, thrusts the ribs into one's stomach, and fosters a general debility."

"As travelers rejoice to see their home country, so also is the end of a book to those who toil."

Even so, without the work of the faithful copyists, we would not have the Christian Scriptures today. As one scribe aptly noted: "There is no scribe who will not pass away, but what his hands have written will remain forever."

If you truly want your work to last, do work that touches the eternal truth and nature of God.

"Store up for yourselves treasures in heaven, where moth and rust do not desroy, and where thieves do not break in and steal."
MATTHEW 6:20 NIV

A young man once made an appointment with a well-published author. The first question the author asked him was, "Why did you want to see me?"

The young man stammered, "Well, I'm a writer, too. I was hoping you could share with me some of your secrets for successful writing."

The author asked a second question, "What have you written?"

"Nothing" the young man replied. "At least nothing that is finished yet."

> Every man's work, whether it be literature, or music, or pictures, or architecture, or anything else, is always a portrait of himself.

The author asked a third question, "Well, if you haven't written, then tell me, what are you *writing?*"

The young man replied, "Well, I'm in school right now so I'm not writing anything at present."

The author then asked a fourth question, "So why do you call yourself a writer?"

Writers write. Composers compose. Painters paint. Workmen work. What you do to a great extent defines what you are and what you become, and in turn, what you are gives rise to what you do. When what you do *externally* matches with what you are *internally,* you have integrity.

> *As in water face reflects face, so*
> *the heart of man reflects man.*
> PROVERBS 27:19 NASB

> What we do on some great occasion will probably
> depend on what we already are; and what we are
> will be the result of previous years of self-discipline.

During a homecoming football game against rival Concordia, Augsburg College found itself losing miserably. But late in the fourth quarter, noseguard David Stevens came off the bench and sparked a fire. He initiated or assisted in two tackles, and when a Concordia player fumbled the ball, David fell on it. As he held the recovered ball high, the crowd roared. It was an unforgettable moment for Augsburg fans!

David Lee Stevens was born to a woman who had taken thalidomide, and his feet appeared where his legs should have started. Abandoned by his mother, David was adopted by a foster family. Bee and Bill Stevens imposed strict rules of behavior on David, nurtured him, and loved him. They insisted he learn to do things for himself, and they never put him in a wheelchair. At age 3, he was fitted with "legs." In school, David became a student leader, made good grades, organized special events, and befriended new students. In high school, he not only played football, but baseball, basketball, and hockey. He became a champion wrestler. When offered handicap license plates, he refused them, stating simply, "Those are for people who need them. I am *not* 'disabled.'"

*I keep under my body, and
bring it into subjection.*
1 CORINTHIANS 9:27

In the fourth round of a national spelling bee in Washington, eleven-year-old Rosalie Elliot, a champion from South Carolina, was asked to spell the word *avowal*. Her soft Southern accent made it difficult for the judges to determine if she had used an *a* or an *e* as the next to the last letter of the word. They deliberated for several minutes and also listened to tape recording playbacks, but still they couldn't determine which letter had been pronounced. Finally the chief judge, John Lloyd, put the question to the only person who knew the answer. He asked Rosalie, "Was the letter an *a* or an *e?*"

> Our deeds determine us, as much as we determine our deeds.

Rosalie, surrounded by whispering young spellers, knew by now the correct spelling of the word. But without hesitation, she replied that she had misspelled the word and had used an *e*.

As she walked from the stage, the entire audience stood and applauded her honesty and integrity, including dozens of newspaper reporters covering the event. While Rosalie had not won the contest, she had definitely emerged a winner that day.

We often think that who we *are* determines what we *do*. Equally true, what you *do* today will determine, in part, who you *are* tomorrow.

Even a child is known by his actions, by whether his conduct is pure and right.
PROVERBS 20:11 NIV

What you do speaks so loud that
I cannot hear what you say.

During the Korean war, a South Korean civilian was arrested by the communists and ordered to be shot. When the young communist leader learned that the prisoner in his charge was the head of an orphanage caring for young children, he decided to spare him . . . but he ordered instead the execution of the man's son. The 19-year-old young man was shot in the presence of his father.

After the war, the young communist leader was captured by the United Nations forces, tried, and condemned to death. But before the sentence could be carried out, the Christian whose son had been killed pleaded for the life of the killer. He argued that the communist had been young when he ordered the execution and that he really didn't know what he was doing. "Give him to me," the man requested, "and I will train him."

The United Nations forces granted the unusual request and the father took the murderer of his son into his own home and cared for him. That young communist became a Christian pastor.

For good or for bad, what we do speaks. How vital it is that we say what we do and do what we say.

*Show me your faith without deeds, and
I will show you my faith by what I do.*
JAMES 2:18 NIV

To crack the lily-white system of higher education in Georgia in the 1960s, black leaders decided they needed to find only two "squeaky-clean students" who couldn't be challenged on moral, intellectual, or educational grounds.

In a discussion about who might be chosen, Alfred Holmes immediately volunteered his son, Hamilton, the top black male senior in the city. Charlayne Hunter-Gault also stepped forward and expressed an interest in applying to the university. Georgia delayed admitting both boys on grounds it had no room in its dormitories, and the matter eventually ended up in federal court. Judge Bootle ordered the university to admit the two, who were qualified in every respect, and thus,

> All virtue is summed up in dealing justly.

segregation ended at the university level in that state, and soon, the nation.

Attorney General Robert Kennedy declared in a speech not long after: "We know that it is the law which enables men to live together, that creates order out of chaos. . . . And we know that if *one* man's rights are denied, the rights of all are endangered."

Justice may be universal, but it always begins at the individual level. Who is it that you might treat more "justly" today?

He hath shewed thee, O man, what is good;
and what doth the LORD require of thee,
but to do justly, and to love mercy,
and to walk humbly with thy God?
MICAH 6:8

> # No matter what a man's past may have been, his future is spotless.

Willingway Hospital is one of the nation's top treatment centers for alcoholism and drug addiction. There would be no Willingway, however, if it weren't for Dot and John, who at one time seemed the least likely candidates to found such a hospital. Early in their courtship, Dot and John drank heavily, and after they married, they began taking amphetamines. John, a medical doctor, was arrested for writing himself narcotics prescriptions. He spent six months in prison, eventually falling on his knees and crying out to God for help in overcoming his addictions.

When John returned to medical practice drug-free and alcohol-free, he began to receive referrals from other doctors to treat their alcoholic patients. Dot and John set up three beds under the chandelier in their own dining room as a detox room. Among their patients have been three of their own four children, each of whom struggled with addictions. As word of their compassion spread, they established a 40-bed hospital on 11 acres close to their home. The chandelier still hangs in the detox room as a symbol of hope. All four children have worked on the medical staff or administration of Willingway. They truly became a family in "full recovery," with God's help.

Forgetting those things which are behind, and reaching forth unto those things which are before, I press toward the mark for the prize of the high calling of God in Christ Jesus.

PHILIPPIANS 3:13-14

Three young men were once given three kernels of corn apiece by a wise old sage, who admonished them to go out into the world and use the corn to bring themselves good fortune.

The first young man put his three kernels of corn into a bowl of hot broth and ate them. The second thought, *I can do better than that,* and he planted his three kernels of corn. Within a few months, he had three stalks of corn. He took the ears of corn from the stalks, boiled them, and had enough corn for three meals.

One of life's great rules is this: The more you give, the more you get.

The third man said to himself, *I can do better than that!* He also planted his three kernels of corn, but when his three stalks of corn produced, he stripped one of the ears and replanted all of the seeds in it, gave the second ear of corn to a sweet maiden, and ate the third. His one full ear's worth of replanted corn kernels gave him 200 stalks of corn! And the kernels of these he continued to replant, setting aside only a bare minimum to eat. He eventually planted a hundred acres of corn. With his fortune, he not only won the hand of the sweet maiden but also purchased the land owned by the sweet maiden's father. And he never hungered again.

The liberal soul shall be made fat:
and he that watereth shall
be watered also himself.
PROVERBS 11:25

> ## Everything comes to him who hustles while he waits.

In 1928, a happy, ambitious young nursing student was diagnosed with tuberculosis. Her family sent her to a nursing home in Saranac Lake for several months of "curing." She was destined to remain in bed for 21 years! Most people would have given up, but not Isabel Smith. She approached the threshold of death on several occasions, but she never ceased to pursue the art of living. She read voraciously, loved to write letters, studied geography, and taught other patients to read and write. From her bed she studied atomic energy with a fellow patient, a young physicist, and organized a town hall on the topic.

While ill, she met a kind, gentle man, also a patient at the sanitarium. She dreamed of marrying him and having a little house "under the mountains." At her lowest ebb, her dream kept her going, and in 1948, she did marry. She then wrote a book about "all the good things life has brought me." *Wish I Might,* published in 1955, earned her enough in royalties to buy her mountain retreat.

A tragic life? Hardly! Isabel Smith achieved everything she set out to achieve, even when the odds against her were 1,000 to 1. Even flat on her back in bed, she never quit growing, learning, and giving.

We do not want you to become lazy, but to imitate those who through faith and patience inherit what has been promised.
HEBREWS 6:12 NIV

According to an old legend, two monks named Tanzan and Ekido were traveling together down a muddy road one day. Heavy monsoon rains had saturated the area and they were grateful for a few moments of sunshine to make their journey. Before long, they came around a bend and encountered a lovely girl in a silk kimono. She looked extremely forlorn as she stared at the muddy road before her.

> A well-trained memory is one that permits you to forget everything that isn't worth remembering.

At once Tanzan responded to her plight. "Come here, girl," he said. Then, lifting her in his arms, he carried her over the slippery ooze and set her down on the other side of the road.

Ekido didn't speak again to Tanzan. It was apparent to Tanzan that something was bothering him deeply, but try as he would, he couldn't get Ekido to talk to him. Then, that night after they reached their intended lodging, Ekido could no longer restrain his anger and disappointment. "We monks don't go near females," he said to Tanzan in an accusing voice. "We especially don't go near young and lovely maidens. It is dangerous. Why did you do that?"

"I left the girl back there, Ekido," replied Tanzan. And then he asked the key question, "Are you still carrying her?"

Finally, brethren, whatsoever things
are true, whatsoever things are honest,
whatsoever things are just. . . .
if there be any virtue, and if there
be any praise, think on these things.
PHILIPPIANS 4:8

> Defeat is not the worst of failures.
>
> Not to have tried is the true failure.

There once was a young man who lived a most miserable life. Orphaned before he was three, he was taken in by strangers. He was kicked out of school, suffered from poverty, and as the result of inherited physical weaknesses, he developed serious heart trouble as a teenager. His beloved wife died early in their marriage. He lived as an invalid most of his adult life and eventually died at the young age of forty. By all outward appearances, he was defeated by life and doomed to be forgotten by history.

Even so, he never quit trying to express himself and to achieve success over the twenty years of his active work life. And in that period, he produced some of the most brilliant articles, essays, and criticisms ever written. His poetry is still read widely and studied by virtually all high school students in the United States. His short stories and detective stories are famous. One of his poems, on display at the Huntington Library, has been valued at more than $50,000, which is far more than the young man earned in his entire lifetime.

His name? Edgar Allan Poe.

Circumstances don't affect your chances for success nearly as much as your level of effort!

Be strong and of a good courage; be not afraid, neither be thou dismayed: for the LORD thy God is with thee whithersoever thou goest.

JOSHUA 1:9

After falling twice in the 1988 Olympic speed-skating races, Dan Jensen sought out sports psychologist Dr. Jim Loehr, who helped him find a new balance between sport and the rest of his life, and who helped him pay more attention to the mental aspects of skating. Peter Mueller became his coach, putting him through workouts that he has since described as "the toughest I've ever known." By the time the 1994 Olympics arrived, Jansen had more confidence than ever. He had set a 500-meter world record just two months previously. That race seemed to be all his!

> Unless you try to do something beyond what you have already mastered, you will never grow.

Then, Jansen fell during the 500-meter race. Dr. Loehr immediately advised, "Start preparing for the 1000. Put the 500 behind you immediately. Stop reliving it." The 1000! For years he didn't believe he could win that distance. He had always considered it his weaker event. Now it was his last chance for an Olympic medal. As the race began, Jansen said, "I just seemed to be sailing along," and then he slipped and came within an inch of stepping on a lane marker. Still, he didn't panic. He raced on and recorded a world-record time that won him the gold medal!

Don't be intimidated by your own goals. Your toughest goal may be linked to your greatest triumph.

Reaching forth unto those things which are before, I press toward the mark for the prize of the high calling of God in Christ Jesus.
PHILIPPIANS 3:13-14

> I don't know the secret to success
> but the key to failure is to
> try to please everyone.

A young man once studied violin under a world-renowned violinist and master teacher. He worked hard for several years at perfecting his talent, and the day finally came when he was called upon to give his first major public recital in the large city where both he and his teacher lived. Following each selection, which he performed with great skill and passion, the performer seemed uneasy about the great applause he received. Even though he knew that those in the audience were musically astute and not likely to give such applause to a less than superior performance, the young man acted almost as if he couldn't hear the appreciation that was being showered upon him.

At the close of the last number, the applause was thunderous, and numerous "Bravos" were shouted. The talented young violinist had his eyes glued, however, on only one spot. Finally, when an elderly man in the first row of the balcony smiled and nodded to him in approval, the young man relaxed and beamed with both relief and joy. His teacher had praised his work! The applause of thousands meant nothing until he had first won the approval of the master.

Who is it that you are trying to please most today?

Am I now trying to win the approval of men, or of God?
GALATIANS 1:10 NIV

The engineers hired to build a suspension bridge across the Niagara River faced a serious problem: how to get the first cable from one side of the river to the next. The river was too wide to throw a cable across it, and too swift to cross by boat.

An engineer finally came up with a solution! With a favoring stiff wind, a kite was lofted and allowed to drift over the river and land on the opposite shore. Attached to the kite was a very light string, which was threaded through the kite's tip so that both ends of the string were in the hands of the kite flyer. Once the kite was in the hands of engineers on the far side, they removed the kite from its string and set up a pulley. A small rope was attached to one end of the original kite string and pullied across

Kites rise highest against the wind, not with it.

the river. At the end of this string, a piece of rope was attached and pullied across . . . and so on, until a cable strong enough to sustain the iron cable which supported the bridge could be drawn across the water.

Let go of your faith. Release it to God, believing that He can and will help you. When you link your released faith with patience and persistence, you will have what it takes to tackle virtually any problem!

When the way is rough, your patience has a chance to grow. So let it grow, and don't try to squirm out of your problems.
JAMES 1:3-4 TLB

> # The secret of success is to be like a duck—smooth and unruffled on top, but paddling furiously underneath.

Wallace E. Johnson, president of Holiday Inns and one of America's most successful builders, once said, "I always keep on a card in my billfold the following verses and refer to them frequently: 'Ask and it shall be given to you: seek and ye shall find: knock and it shall be opened unto you: for every one that asketh receiveth; and he that seeketh findeth; and to him that knocketh, it shall be opened' (Matthew 7:7-8).

"These verses are among God's greatest promises. Yet they are a little one-sided. They indicate a philosophy of receiving but not of giving. One day as my wife, Alma, and I were seeking God's guidance for a personal problem, I came across the following verse which has since been a daily reminder to me of what my responsibility as a businessman is to God: 'Study to shew thyself approved unto God, a workman that needeth not to be ashamed, rightly dividing the word of truth' (2 Timothy 2:15).

"Since then I have measured my actions against the phrase: A workman that needeth not to be ashamed."

FAITH ON THE INSIDE + WORKS ON THE OUTSIDE = A SUCCESSFUL LIFE!

I laboured more abundantly than they all: yet not I, but the grace of God which was with me.
1 CORINTHIANS 15:10

A little boy was once overheard talking to himself as he strutted out of his house into the backyard, carrying a baseball bat and ball. Once in the yard, he tipped his baseball cap to his eager puppy, and picking up the bat and ball, he announced with a loud voice, "I'm the greatest hitter in the world."

He then proceeded to toss the ball into the air, swing at it, and miss. "Strike one!" he cried, as if playing the role of umpire.

He picked up the ball, threw it into the air and said again, "I'm the greatest baseball hitter ever!" And again he swung at the ball and missed. "Strike two!" he announced to his dog and the yard.

Undaunted, he picked up the ball, examined his bat, and then just before tossing the ball

> The cheerful man will do more in the same time, will do it better, will preserve it longer, than the sad or sullen.

into the air, announced once again, "I'm the greatest hitter who ever lived." He swung the bat hard . . . but missed for the third time. "Strike three!" he cried. And then he added, "Wow! What a pitcher! I'm the greatest pitcher in all the world!"

A positive mental attitude goes a long way toward making a day short. It's a big part of making a difficult job seem small.

When a man is gloomy, everything seems to go wrong; when he is cheerful, everything seems right!
PROVERBS 15:15 TLB

Money is a good servant
but a bad master.

Financial advisor and author Ron Blue felt he had everything he needed to be successful at the age of 24—an MBA (Master of Business Administration) degree, a CPA (Certified Public Accountant) certificate, a prestigious position in the New York City office of the world's largest CPA firm. But then at the age of 32, he committed his life to Jesus Christ and he began to see life from a new perspective. When he decided to establish his own financial advisory firm, he used his skills to develop a business plan and arrange for a $10,000 line of credit at a bank. Almost immediately, however, he felt convicted that God did not want him to borrow money to start his business. He canceled the credit line, not knowing what to do next but knowing he was not to go into debt.

One day while explaining his business idea to a friend, the friend said, "Would you consider designing a financial seminar for our executives who are getting ready to retire?" Ron jumped at the opportunity. His friend was the training director for a large company and the company agreed to pay $6,000 in advance for development of the seminar, then $1,000 each for four seminars during the year. Ron had the $10,000 he needed, without borrowing a dime.

Stay out of debt. You'll feel much freer!

The rich ruleth over the poor, and the borrower is servant to the lender.
PROVERBS 22:7

Nelson Diebel, a hyperactive and delinquent child, was enrolled in The Peddie School where he met swimming coach Chris Martin, who believed the more one practices the better one performs. Within a month, he had Nelson swimming 30 to 40 hours a week, even though Nelson could not sit still in a classroom for 15 minutes. Martin saw potential in Nelson. He constantly put new goals in front of him, trying to get him to focus and turn his anger into strength. Nelson eventually qualified for the Junior Nationals, his times qualifying him for Olympic Trials.

> No plan is worth the paper it is printed on unless it starts you doing something.

In a diving accident, however, Nelson broke both hands and arms, and doctors warned he would probably never regain his winning form. Martin said to him, "You're coming all the way back. . . . If you're not committed to that, we're going to stop right now." Nelson agreed, and within weeks after his casts were off, he was swimming again. In 1992, he won Olympic gold. As he accepted his medal, he recalls thinking *I planned and dreamed and worked so hard . . . and I did it!* The kid who once couldn't sit still and who had no ambition . . . had learned to make a plan, pursue it, and achieve it. He had become a winner in far more than swimming.

Be ye doers of the word, and not hearers only, deceiving your own selves.
JAMES 1:22

> Life is a coin. You can spend it
> any way you wish, but you
> can spend it only once.

Head and founder of a major contracting firm, Frank refused to celebrate the holidays, saying only, "Christmas is for children." Then one brisk December day Frank walked to work and in a creche in a department store window, he saw anew the Child. He started to move away, but as he did, a sign across the street caught his attention: "Holy Innocents Home." His mind raced back to a Sunday school lesson years ago about how King Herod had feared the Baby Jesus and slaughtered children in Bethlehem. He recalled the day his own son David had died at the age of 18 months. He hadn't been able to speak his name since.

Frank impulsively went to the library and was surprised to learn as he researched the story that 20 children were estimated to have been killed by Herod's men. He left the library with a mission. Later that night, he told his wife Adele that he had visited the orphanage . . . that he had given them some money . . . that they were going to build a wing with it . . . and then he said, "They are going to name it for David." What Frank didn't tell his wife was that he had a vision of 20 children playing in a bright new wing at Holy Innocents. As Adele hugged him, the vision came again, but this time there were 21 children at play.

It is appointed unto men once to die,
but after this the judgment.
HEBREWS 9:27

The German sculptor Dannaker worked for two years on a statue of Christ until it looked perfect to him. He called a little girl into his studio, and pointing to the statue, asked her, "Who is that?" The little girl promptly replied, "A great man."

Dannaker was disheartened. He took his chisel and began anew. For six long years he toiled. Again, he invited a little girl into his workshop, stood her before the figure, and said, "Who is that?" She looked up at it for a moment, and then tears welled in her eyes and she folded her hands across her chest and said, "Suffer the little children to come unto me" (Mark 10:14). This time Dannaker knew he had succeeded.

> Only passions, great passions, can elevate the soul to great things.

The sculptor later confessed that during those six years, Christ had revealed Himself to him in a vision, and he had only transferred to the marble what he had seen with his inner eyes.

Later, when Napoleon Bonaparte asked him to make a statue of Venus for the Louvre, Dannaker refused. "A man," he said, "who had seen Christ can never employ his gifts in carving a pagan goddess. My art is henceforth a consecrated thing."

The true value of a work comes not from effort, nor its completion, but from Christ who inspires it.

Be. . . fervent in spirit; serving the Lord.
Romans 12:10-11

191

> # Failures want pleasing methods;
> # successes want pleasing results.

Sadie Delaney's father taught her always to strive to do better than her competition. She proved the value of that lesson shortly before she received her teaching license. A supervisor came to watch her and two other student teachers. Their assignment was to teach a class to bake cookies. Since the supervisor didn't have time for each teacher to go through the entire lesson, she divided the lesson and Sadie was assigned to teach the girls how to serve and clean up.

The first student teacher panicked and forgot to halve the recipe and preheat the oven. The second girl was so behind because of the first girl's errors that the students made a mess in forming and baking the cookies.

Then it was Sadie's turn. She said to the girls, "Listen, we have to work together as a team." They quickly baked the remaining dough. Several girls were lined up to scrub the pans as soon as the cookies came out of the oven. Within ten minutes, they had several dozen perfect cookies and a clean kitchen. The supervisor was so impressed that she offered Sadie a substitute teacher's license on the spot and she soon became the first black person ever to teach domestic science in New York City's public high schools.

Do what it takes to get right results.

No discipline seems pleasant at the time, but painful. Later on, however, it produces a harvest of righteousness and peace for those who have been trained by it.
HEBREWS 12:11 NIV

A man once sat down to have dinner with his family. Before they began to eat, the family members joined hands around the table and the man said a prayer, thanking God for the food, the hands that had prepared it, and for the source of all life.

During the meal, however, he complained at length about the staleness of the bread, the bitterness of the coffee, and a bit of mold he found on one edge of the brick of cheese.

His young daughter asked him, "Daddy, do you think God heard you say grace before the meal?"

> Once a word has been allowed to escape, it cannot be recalled.

"Of course, honey," he answered confidently.

Then she asked, "Do you think God heard everything that was said during dinner?" The man answered, "Why, yes, I believe so. God hears everything."

She thought for a moment and then asked, "Daddy, which do you think God believed?"

Truly, the Lord hears everything we say during the day, not only those words that are addressed specifically to Him. Make everything you say today worthy of His overhearing!

Let no corrupt communication proceed out of your mouth, but that which is good to the use of edifying, that it may minister grace unto the hearers.
Ephesians 4:29

> Most of the things worth doing in the
> world had been declared impossible
> before they were done.

Many resisted new ideas and inventions that we now consider commonplace:

For example, in Germany, "experts" proved that if trains went as fast as 15 miles an hour—considered a frightful speed—blood would spurt from the travelers' noses and passengers would suffocate when going through tunnels. In the United States, experts said the introduction of the railroad would require the building of many insane asylums since people would be driven mad with terror at the sight of locomotives.

The New York YWCA announced typing lessons for women in 1881, and vigorous protests erupted on the grounds that the female constitution would break down under the strain.

When the idea of iron ships was proposed, experts insisted that they would not float, would damage more easily than wooden ships when grounding, that it would be difficult to preserve the iron bottom from rust, and that iron would play havoc with compass readings.

Ideas that propel us forward can be seen as difficult changes. When we're open to God's creative heart, the results are beyond our imagination. What is He prompting you to change in your life today?

"With God all things are possible."
MATTHEW 19:26

During the darkest days of the Civil War, the hopes of the Union nearly died. When certain goals seemed unreachable, the leaders of the Union turned to President Abraham Lincoln for solace, guidance, and renewal of hope. Once when a delegation called at the White House and detailed a long list of crises facing the nation, Lincoln told this story:

Years ago a young friend and I were out one night when a shower of meteors fell from the clear November sky. The young man was frightened, but I told him to look up in the sky past the shooting stars to the fixed stars beyond, shining serene in the firmament, and I said, "Let us not mind the meteors, but let us keep our eyes on the stars."

Obstacles are those frightful things you see when you take your eyes off the goal.

When times are troubled or life seems to be changing greatly, keep your inner eyes of faith and hope on those things that you know to be lasting and sure. God alone—and a relationship with Him that is eternal—is the Supreme Goal. God never changes and He cannot be removed from His place as the King of Glory.

Peter. . . . walked on the water toward Jesus. But when he looked around at the high waves, he was terrified and began to sink.
MATTHEW 14:29-30 TLB

A good reputation is more valuable than money.

In *Up from Slavery,* Booker T. Washington describes meeting an ex-slave from Virginia:

"I found that this man had made a contract with his master, two or three years previous to the Emancipation Proclamation, to the effect that the slave was to be permitted to buy himself, by paying so much per year for his body; and while he was paying for himself, he was to be permitted to labor where and for whom he pleased.

"Finding that he could secure better wages in Ohio, he went there. When freedom came, he was still in debt to his master some $300. Notwithstanding that the Emancipation Proclamation freed him from any obligation to his master, this black man walked the greater portion of the distance back to where his old master lived in Virginia, and placed the last dollar, with interest, in his hands.

"In talking to me about this, the man told me that he knew that he did not have to pay his debt, but that he had given his word to his master, and his word he had never broken. He felt that he could not enjoy his freedom till he had fulfilled his promise."

Your ability to keep your word, not your ability to acquire money, is your true measure as a person.

A good name is rather to be chosen than great riches.
PROVERBS 22:1

A janitor at the First Security Bank in Boise, Idaho, once accidentally put a box of 8,000 checks worth $840,000 on a trash table, which the operator of the paper shredder dutifully dumped into his machine that night, cutting the checks into quarter-inch shreds. He then dumped the paper scraps into a garbage can outside the bank. When the bank supervisor realized what happened the next morning, he moaned, "I wanted to cry."

> An error doesn't become a mistake until you refuse to correct it.

Most of the checks had been cashed at the bank and were awaiting shipment to a clearing-house. Their loss represented a bookkeeping nightmare since most of the checks were still unrecorded, and as a result, the bankers could not know who paid what to whom.

What did the supervisor do? He ordered that the shredded pieces be reconstructed. And so, fifty employees worked in two shifts for six hours a day inside six rooms—shifting, matching, and pasting the pieces together as if they were jigsaw puzzles—until all 8,000 of the checks were "put together again."

Humpty Dumpty may have fallen from the wall, but did the king's men even try to put him together again? If you make a mistake, at least put forth the effort to find a solution.

He who heeds discipline shows the
way to life, but whoever ignores
correction leads others astray.
PROVERBS 10:17 NIV

> ## Hating people is like burning down your own house to get rid of a rat.

After two years in the Navy, Willard Scott returned to his old job with NBC radio, but to a new supervisor. Willard found himself at odds with his new boss at every turn, and he was furious when he rescheduled "Joy Boys," a comedy show he did with Eddie Walker, for the worst slot on radio—eight to midnight. Willard was braced for a change-or-I'll-leave confrontation when he recalled Proverbs 19:11: "To be patient shows intelligence; to overlook faults is a man's glory." He and Eddie decided to work themselves to the bone and within three years they made "Joy Boys" the top-rated show in Washington.

Willard says, "I learned that I, too, had been wrong. In all my dealings with my boss, I had aggravated the problem. I knew he didn't like me, and in response I was barely civil to him and dodged him as much as I could. But one day he invited me to a station party I couldn't avoid. There I met his fiancée. She was bright, alive, and down-to-earth. *How could a woman like that care for anybody who didn't have something to recommend him? . . .* I was able to get new insight into my boss's character. As time went on my attitude changed, and so did his." Willard and his boss became friends, and he remained at NBC.

If ye bite and devour one another,
take heed that ye be not
consumed one of another.
GALATIANS 5:15

A missionary from Sweden was once urged by his friends to give up his idea of returning to India because it was so hot there. "Man," the fellow Swede urged, as if telling his friend something he didn't already know, "it's 120 degrees in the shade in that country!" The Swedish missionary replied, "Vell, ve don't always have to stay in the shade, do ve?"

Humor is not a sin. It is a God-given escape hatch. Being able to see the lighter side of life is a virtue. And indeed, every vocation and behavior of life has a lighter side, if we are only willing to see it. Wholesome humor can do a great deal to help defuse a tense, heated situation.

In developing a good sense of humor, we must be able to laugh at our own mistakes;

> Laughter is the sun that drives winter from the human face.

accept justified criticism—and recover from it; and learn to avoid using statements that are unsuitable—even though they may be funny.

James M. Gray and William Houghton—two Godly men—were praying together one day, and the elderly Dr. Gray concluded his prayer by saying: "Lord, keep me cheerful. Keep me from becoming a cranky, old man." Keeping a sense of humor is a great way to avoid becoming a bitter, impatient, critical person.

A merry heart maketh a cheerful
countenance: but by sorrow of
the heart the spirit is broken.
PROVERBS 15:13

> Good nature begets smiles,
> smiles beget friends, and friends
> are better than a fortune.

Most families receive at least one Christmas card each year. Millions of cards are mailed each holiday season, worldwide. Have you ever wondered where this custom began?

A museum director in the mid-19th century had a personal habit of sending notes to his friends at Christmastime each year, just to wish them a joyful holiday season. One year, he found he had little time to write and yet he still wanted to send a message of good cheer. He asked his friend, John Horsely, to design a card that he might sign and send. Those who received the cards loved them and created cards of their own. And thus, the Christmas card was invented!

It's often the simple heartfelt gestures in life that speak most loudly of friendship. Ask yourself today: *What can I do to bring a smile to the face of a friend? What can I do to bring good cheer into the life of someone who is in need, trouble, sickness, or sorrow?* Follow through on your answer. It's not a gift you are giving as much as a friendship you are building.

The light in the eyes [of him whose heart is joyful] rejoices the hearts of others.
PROVERBS 15:30 AMP

He received a medical degree from New York University College of Medicine. He received an appointment to the Virus Research Laboratory at the University of Pittsburgh. He received an assignment from the army to develop a vaccine against influenza. And among the many honors he has received was a Presidential Medal of Freedom.

Jonas Salk, however, is not known for what he received, but for what he gave. He and his team of researchers gave their efforts to prepare an inactivated polio virus that could serve as an immunizing agent against polio. By 1952, they had created a vaccine, and in 1955 the vaccine was released for widespread use in the United States, virtually ending the ravaging crippling effects of polio.

No person was ever honored for what he received. Honor has been the reward for what he gave.

You will receive many opportunities in your life, and very likely, a number of certificates, diplomas, or awards of various types. What will ultimately count, however, is what you do with the training you have received and the skills and traits you have developed.

Find a way to give, create, or generate something today that will benefit others. In that is not only a potential for fame and reward, but also great personal satisfaction—the reward of highest value.

The righteous give without sparing.
PROVERBS 21:26 NIV

> The difference between the right word
> and the almost right word is the difference
> between lightning and the lightning bug.

Consider the "infamous" statements listed below. And note as you read that they all could be *corrected* by changing or inserting only one word in each quote!

"Everything that can be invented has been invented." Charles H. Duell, U.S. Patent Office director, 1899

"Who wants to hear actors talk?" H.M. Warner, Warner Brothers Pictures, © 1927

"Sensible and responsible women do not want to vote." Grover Cleveland, 1905

"There is no likelihood man can ever tap the power of the atom." Robert Millikan, Nobel prize winner in physics, 1923

"Heavier-than-air flying machines are impossible." Lord Kelvin, president, Royal Society, © 1895

"[Babe] Ruth made a big mistake when he gave up pitching." Tris Speaker, 1927

"Gone with the Wind is going to be the biggest flop in Hollywood history." Gary Cooper

To be only one word off can make a big difference.

*A word fitly spoken is like apples
of gold in pictures of silver.*
PROVERBS 25:11

A feud developed between two families who lived side by side in the mountains of Kentucky. It started when Grandpa Smith's cow jumped a stone fence and ate Grandpa Brown's corn. Brown shot the cow. A Smith boy then shot *two* Brown boys. The Browns shot one Smith. Bill Brown planned to kill a second Smith, but before he could, he was called away to war. While he was away, Bill's mother had a hard time making ends meet for her family, since it was Bill's father who was had been one of the victims.

> This world belongs to the man who is wise enough to change his mind in the presence of facts.

At Christmas the head of the Smith clan took his family to church. Usually he stayed outside, but this year it was so cold he went in to wait. The sermon was on Christ, the Prince of Peace, who died on *our* place for *our* sins. It struck him hard. He realized what a crime he had committed, repented, and then secretly hired a young boy to carry a basket of food to the Brown's home every day until Bill returned.

Once home, Bill set out to discover who had so generously helped his family. He followed the boy to the Smith's house, where Smith met him and said, "Shoot me, Bill, if you want to. But Christ has already died for my sins and I hope you'll forgive me, too." Bill did, and neighbors truly became neighbors again.

> *Whoever heeds correction*
> *gains understanding.*
> PROVERBS 15:32 NIV

> Blessed is the man who is too
> busy to worry in the daytime and
> too sleepy to worry at night.

Opera star Marguerite Piazza was at the height of her career, married to a devoted husband, mother of six healthy children. And then her world seemed to turn upside down. Her husband died suddenly and soon after, a spot on her cheek was diagnosed as melanoma, a deadly type of cancer. She was told that a disfiguring surgery to remove her cheek was her only hope for survival. The same day she received that news, she was scheduled to sing to a sell-out audience. She says, "What do you do at a time like that? You do what you are paid to do, and I was paid to lift people with my talent. So, as I stood in the wings of the opera house, I prayed. Then I hung my troubles on a hanger and left them in the closet." She performed her heart out, and even after her surgery, she remained beautiful, raised her family, and continued to sing!

Rather than hang his worries in a closet, a man took another approach. He put them in a box. Each time he had a worry, he'd write it down and deposit it. Then, on Worry Wednesday, he read the contents of his box. To his amazement, most of the things he had worried about had already been resolved. He soon discarded the box!

Worry doesn't pay. It only bogs you down.

The sleep of a labouring man is sweet.
ECCLESIASTES 5:12

A farmer once caught a young eagle in the forest, brought it home, and raised it among his ducks and turkeys. Five years later, a naturalist came to visit him and saw the bird. "That's an eagle, not a chicken!" he said. "Yes," said the farmer, "but I've raised it to be a chicken." "Still," said the naturalist, "it has a wing span of fifteen feet. It's an eagle!" "It will never fly," said the farmer. The naturalist disagreed and they decided to put their argument to the test.

Every calling is great when greatly pursued.

First, the naturalist picked up the eagle and said, "Eagle, thou art an eagle; thou doest belong to the sky and not to this earth; stretch forth thy wings and fly." The eagle saw the chickens and jumped down. The next day the naturalist took the eagle to the top of the house, said the same thing, and let the eagle go. Again, it spotted the chickens below and fluttered down to join them in feeding.

"One more try," said the naturalist. He took the eagle up a mountain. The trembling bird looked around, and then the naturalist made it look into the sun. Suddenly, the eagle stretched out its wings, gave a mighty screech, and flew away, never to return.

People may say you are just a hunk of flesh. But deep inside, you have a spirit created in God's image!

I press toward the mark for the prize of the high calling of God in Christ Jesus.
PHILIPPIANS 3:14

> Treat everybody alike, no matter from what station in life he comes. . . . really great men and women are those who are natural, frank, and honest with everyone with whom they come into contact.

In ancient Greece, the philosopher Aristippus—considered by all who knew him to be the master of political craftiness—learned to get along well in royal circles by flattering the tyrant Denys. Not only did he flatter Denys, but he was proud that he did. In fact, Aristippus disdained less prosperous fellow philosophers and wise men who refused to stoop that low.

One day Aristippus saw his colleague Diogenes washing vegetables and he said to him, "If you would only learn to flatter King Denys you would not have to be washing lentils." Diogenes looked up slowly and replied, "And you, if you had only learned to live on lentils, would not have to flatter King Denys."

Another way to regard flattery is this:

F—foolish
L—laughable
A—accolades
T—to
T—tell
E—everyone
R—'round
Y—you

Speak the truth sincerely. And when the truth is painful, consider the option of remaining silent!

Don't show favoritism.
JAMES 2:1 NIV

Coach Gregory watched with pride as Rashaan Salaam accepted the Heisman trophy. He recalled the hotshot 18-year-old who, finally free from his mother's tight discipline, had arrived in Colorado ready to devour the world. He says, "Rashaan was a gangster wannabe. He came here wearing all this red stuff, talking about gangs. He hadn't done it back home because his mother would have never tolerated it." And neither did Gregory. He never lectured or preached to Rashaan, but he did ask him questions. When Rashaan came to him talking about his new friends, Gregory said, "Sure, they are your friends, but are you their friend? They know what you're trying to accomplish. They know the potential you have to do great things. If you are their friend, when they

'Tis better to be alone than in bad company.

get ready to get into something, they'll say, 'Salaam, get out of here. Go home and study.'"

As a coach, Gregory wanted Salaam to "find daylight" and get into the end zone, but as a friend, he wanted him to live in the daylight and make it to life's goal lines as a productive citizen. Winning a football game is never a one-man-only effort. It's a team effort. The same holds true for life, and the good news is, you can choose the players on your team!

Do not be misled: "Bad company corrupts good character."
1 CORINTHIANS 15:33 NIV

The rotten apple spoils
his companion.

In his book *The Mind of Watergate*, a psychiatrist Leo Rangell, M.D., relates what he calls a "compromise of integrity" as he analyzes the relationship between former President Richard M. Nixon and several of his closest confidants. He records a conversation between investigative committee member Senator Howard Baker and young Herbert L. Porter.

Baker: "Did you ever have any qualms about what you were doing? . . . did you ever think of saying, 'I do not think this is quite right.' . . . Did you ever think of that?"

Porter: "Yes, I did."

Baker: "What did you do about it?"

Porter: "I did not do anything."

Baker: "Why didn't you?"

Porter: "In all honesty, probably because of the fear of the group pressure that would ensue, of not being a team player."

There's nothing wrong with being a team player, as long as you are very careful about choosing your team! You will become like your friends, even as they change and become a little more like you. Therefore, choose your friends cautiously and thoughtfully!

He that walketh with wise men shall be wise: but a companion of fools shall be destroyed.
PROVERBS 13:20

225

We often think of great artists and musicians as having "bursts" of genius. More often, they are models of painstaking patience. Their greatest works tend to have been accomplished over long periods, and often through extreme hardships.

Beethoven is said to have rewritten each bar of his music at least a dozen times.

Josef Haydn produced more than 800 musical compositions before writing "The Creation," the oratorio for which he is most famous.

Patience is bitter but its fruit is sweet.

Michelangelo's "Last Judgment" is considered one of the twelve master paintings of the ages. It took him eight years to complete. He produced more than 2,000 sketches and renderings in the process.

Leonardo da Vinci worked on "The Last Supper" for ten years, often working so diligently that he forgot to eat.

When he was quite elderly, the pianist Ignace Paderewski was asked by an admirer, "Is it true that you still practice every day?" He replied, "Yes, at least six hours a day." The admirer said in awe, "You must have a world of patience." Paderewski said, "I have no more patience than the next fellow. I just use mine."

Ye have need of patience, that,
after ye have done the will of God,
ye might receive the promise.
HEBREWS 10:36

> The greedy search for money or success will almost always lead men into unhappiness. Why? Because that kind of life makes them depend upon things outside themselves.

Few people have undergone the trials and tribulations of Aleksandr Solzhenitsyn, who suffered decades of horrendous hardship as a political exile in the Siberian prison system known as the "gulag." We can learn from Solzhenitsyn not only because he is a survivor, but because he has been in a situation that few of us have ever known—an existence of near total deprivation. He has not only lived without luxuries, but without necessities.

He writes as few can in *The Prison Chronicle:*

Don't be afraid of misfortune and do not yearn after happiness. It is, after all, all the same. The bitter doesn't last forever, and the sweet never fills the cup to overflowing. It is enough if you don't freeze in the cold and if hunger and thirst don't claw at your sides. If your back isn't broken, if your feet can walk, if both arms work, if both eyes can see, and if both ears can hear, then whom should you envy? And why? Our envy of others devours us most of all. Rub your eyes and purify your heart and prize above all else in the world those who love you and wish you well.

Make sure that your character is free from the love of money, being content with what you have; for He Himself has said, "I will never desert you, nor will I ever forsake you."
HEBREWS 13:5 NASB

A little girl named Mary had come home from a tough day at school. She stretched herself out on the living room sofa to have her own private pity party. She moaned to her mom and brother, "Nobody loves me . . . the whole world hates me!"

Her brother, busily occupied with his video game, hardly looked her way as he passed on this encouraging word: "That's not true, Mary. Some people don't even know you."

Mary, no doubt, was *not* amused. She probably wished her brother had heeded the advice of William Penn, founding leader of the colony that became Pennsylvania. He had these rules for conversation: "Avoid company where it is not profitable or necessary, and in those occasions, speak

> Not only to say the right thing in the right place, but far more difficult, to leave unsaid the wrong thing at the tempting moment.

little, and last. Silence is wisdom where speaking is folly, and always safe. Some are so foolish as to interrupt and anticipate those that speak instead of hearing and thinking before they answer, which is uncivil, as well as silly. If thou thinkest twice before thou speakest once, thou wilt speak twice the better for it. Better to say nothing than not to the purpose. And to speak pertinently, consider both what is fit, and when it is fit, to speak. In all debates, let truth be thy aim, not victory or an unjust interest; and endeavor to gain, rather than to expose, thy antagonist."

Self-control means controlling the tongue!
A quick retort can ruin everything.
PROVERBS 13:3 TLB

School seeks to get you ready for examination; life gives the finals.

The Koh-i-noor diamond is among the world's most spectacular. It is part of the British crown jewels, presented to Queen Victoria by a maharajah in India when the maharajah was only a young boy.

Years later, as a grown man, the maharajah visited Queen Victoria in England. He asked that the stone be brought from the Tower of London, where it was kept in safety, to Buckingham Palace. The queen did as he requested.

Taking the diamond in his hand, he knelt before the queen and presented it back to her, saying, "Your Majesty, I gave this jewel when I was a child, too young to know what I was doing. I want to give it to you again in the fullness of my strength, with all of my heart and affection, and gratitude, now and forever, fully realizing all that I do."

A day will come when you likely will look back and say, "I'm grateful for my teachers, and the lessons they taught me about discipline, concentration, hard work, cooperation, and the right and wrong ways to compete." Even more valuable will be the day when you look in a mirror and say, "Knowing what I now know about my life, I see value in continuing to teach these lessons to myself."

Examine yourselves to see whether you are in the faith; test yourselves.
2 CORINTHIANS 13:5 NIV

The Sixty-four Thousand Dollar Question was the hottest show on television in 1955. The more Joyce watched the program, the more she thought, *I could do that*. At the time, Joyce had quit her teaching job to raise her daughter, and she and her husband were living on $50 a month. She didn't dream of winning the top prize—*any* prize at that point would have helped greatly.

So, as a psychologist by training, Joyce analyzed the show. She saw that each contestant had a built-in incongruity—the Marine who was a gourmet cook, the shoemaker who knew about opera. She found herself a short, blond psychologist and mother with no incongruity. She decided after some thought to become an expert in boxing! She ate, drank, and slept

> Diligence is the mother of good fortune.

boxing, studying its statistics, personalities, and history. When she felt she was ready, she applied for the show, was accepted, and won . . . and won . . . until she won the $64,000 prize. The experience led her to a dream career as a television journalist who could translate the results of psychological research into terms that people could use in their everyday lives. Once she saw that possibility, there was no stopping Dr. Joyce Brothers.

The plans of the diligent lead to profit.
PROVERBS 21:5 NIV

> The road to success is dotted with
> many tempting parking places.

The first things to emerge at a baby giraffe's birth are its front hooves and head. Minutes later, the newborn falls ten feet from its mother's body and lands on its back. Within seconds, it rolls to an upright position with its legs tucked under its body. From this position, it views the world for the first time and shakes off any remaining birthing fluid.

The mother giraffe lowers her head just long enough to take a quick look at her calf and then she does what seems to be a very unreasonable thing: she kicks her baby, sending it sprawling head over heels. If it doesn't get up, she kicks it again and again until the calf finally stands on its wobbly legs. And then what does the mother giraffe do? She kicks it off its feet! Why? She wants it to remember how it got up.

In the wild, baby giraffes must be able to get up as quickly as possible to stay with the herd and avoid becoming a meal for lions, hyenas, leopards, and wild hunting dogs. The best way a mother giraffe has of ensuring that her calf lives is for her to teach it to "get up quickly and get with it."

Don't complain if those who love you push you into action. They are doing you a favor.

Let us lay aside every weight, and the sin which doth so easily beset us, and let us run with patience the race that is set before us.

HEBREWS 12:1

On May 21, 1946, a scientist at Los Alamos was carrying out a necessary experiment in preparation for an atomic test to be conducted in the waters of the South Pacific. He had successfully performed this experiment many times before. It involved pushing two hemispheres of uranium together to determine the amount of a U-235 needed for a chain reaction—the amount scientists call "a critical mass." Just as the mass became critical, he would push the hemispheres apart with his screwdriver, instantly stopping the chain reaction.

> When you are laboring for others, let it be with the same zeal as if it were for yourself.

That day, however, just as the material became critical, the screwdriver slipped. The hemispheres of uranium came too close together, and instantly the room was filled with a dazzling bluish haze. Young Louis Slotin, instead of ducking and thereby possibly saving himself, tore the two hemispheres apart with his hands, thus interrupting the chain reaction.

In this instant, self-forgetful act, he saved the lives of seven other persons in the room. He, however, died in agony nine days later.

With the same energy that you would do something for yourself . . . do something for someone else today!

Each of you should look not only to your own interests, but also to the interests of others.
PHILIPPIANS 2:4 NIV

> The Bible knows nothing of a hierarchy of labor.
>
> No work is degrading.
>
> If it ought to be done, then it is good work.

When David was 12, he convinced a restaurant manager that he was actually 16 and was hired as a lunch-counter waiter for 25 cents an hour. The place was owned by two Greek immigrant brothers, Frank and George, who had started their lives in America as a dishwasher and a hot dog seller. David noted that they set high standards and never asked anything of their employees that they wouldn't do themselves. Frank once told David, "As long as you try you can always work for me. But when you don't try, you can't work for me." Trying meant everything from working hard to treating customers politely. Once when Frank noticed a waitress giving a customer a rough time, he fired her on the spot and waited on the table himself. David determined that would never happen to him!

The usual tip for waiters in those days was a dime, but David discovered that if he brought out the food quickly and was especially polite, he sometimes got a quarter as a tip. He set a goal to see how many customers he could wait on in one night. His record was 100!

R. David Thomas, better known as "Dave," was the founder and senior chairman of Wendy's International, Inc., a chain of 6,000 restaurants.

To rejoice in his labour;
this is the gift of God.
ECCLESIASTES 5:19

McCormick's father was what many might call a "tinkerer." A mechanical genius, he invented many farm devices. Sadly, however, he became the laughingstock of his community for attempting to make a grain-cutting device. For years he worked on the project but never succeeded in getting it to operate reliably.

In spite of the discouragements of his father and the ridicule of neighbors, young McCormick took up the old machine as his own project. He also experienced years of experiment and failure. And then, one day he succeeded in constructing a reaper that would harvest grain!

Even so, jealous opposition prevented the invention from being used for a number of

The ripest peach is highest on the tree.

years. McCormick was able to make sales only after he gave a personal guarantee to each purchaser that the reaper would do the job he claimed it could do. Finally, after decades of trial and error, hoping and waiting, a firm in Cincinnati agreed to manufacture 100 machines. The famous McCormick reaper was "born."

To get to the ripest peach on the highest branch, you need to climb one limb at a time and not be defeated by the scrape of bark, the occasional fall, and the frequent feeling of being left dangling!

Let us not become weary in doing good, for at the proper time we will reap a harvest if we do not give up.
GALATIANS 6:9 NIV

> When you do the things you have to do
> when you have to do them, the day will
> come when you can do the things you
> want to do when you want to do them.

The bee is often described as being "busy." It deserves this adjective! To produce one pound of honey, a bee must visit 56,000 clover heads. Since each head has 60 flower tubes, a bee must make a total of 3,360,000 visits. In the process, the average bee would travel the equivalent of three times around the world.

To make just one *tablespoon* of honey, the amount that might go on a biscuit, a little bee must make 4,200 trips to the flowers, averaging about ten trips each day, each trip lasting approximately 20 minutes. It visits 400 different flowers.

Day in, day out, the work of a bee is fairly unglamorous. It flies, it takes in nectar, it flies, it deposits nectar. But, in the process, it produces, and what it produces creates a place for it in the hive.

You may think your daily chores are a waste of your time. But, in fact, your doing of those chores is "making" you. One day you won't even have to think, *I must get disciplined. I must get to work. I must stick with it.* If you have done your chores faithfully and to the best of your ability, the chores will have become a part of the way you tackle every challenge the rest of your life.

He becometh poor that dealeth with a slack hand: but the hand of the diligent maketh rich.
PROVERBS 10:4

Dr. Ashley Montagu met two young men shortly after the end of World War II. They had spent two years in Auschwitz, the cruel death camp operated by the Nazis. Prior to Auschwitz they had lived in Vienna in a cellar where they had been kept hidden by Christian friends. All of the others housed with them in the cellar had been exterminated solely because they were Jews. After the war ended, these two men had walked from Vienna to Berlin, hoping to find relatives there. There, they were picked up by an American Jewish soldier who brought them to America. Both of them wanted to become physicians and that's how Dr. Montagu, a professor in a medical school, came to meet them. Noting that "they didn't exhibit any of the scars that one might

> A man without mirth is like a wagon without springs; he is jolted disagreeably by every pebble in the road.

have expected from their unhappy existence," he asked them how they came to be such cheerful people.

They replied, "A group of us decided that no matter what happened, it wouldn't get us down." They told him they had attempted to be cheerful regardless of their circumstances, never yielding for a moment to the idea that they were either inferior or doomed.

They were living proof to Dr. Montagu that even under impossible conditions, it's possible to be happy!

A merry heart doeth good like a medicine: but a broken spirit drieth the bones.
PROVERBS 17:22

The 2 most important words: "Thank you."
The most important word: "We."
The least important word: "I."

There's an old saying that goes, "It needs more skill than I can tell, to play the second fiddle well."

Along that line, Leonard Bernstein was once asked which instrument was the most difficult to play. He thought for a moment and said, "The second fiddle. I can get plenty of first violinists, but to find someone who can play the second fiddle with enthusiasm—that's a problem. And if we have no second fiddle, we have no harmony."

General Robert E. Lee was a man who knew the value of playing second fiddle. This great general never stopped being a true southern gentleman. Once, while riding on a train to Richmond, he was seated at the rear of the car and all the other places were filled with officers and soldiers. An elderly woman, poorly dressed, boarded the coach at a rural station. Finding no seat offered to her, she trudged down the aisle toward the back of the car. Immediately, Lee stood up and offered her his place. One after another of the men then arose and offered the general his seat. "No, gentlemen," he replied. "if there is none for this lady, there can be none for me!"

Genuine humility is what prompts us to say a heartfelt thank-you and to favor others over ourselves.

Don't be selfish. . . . Be humble, thinking of others as better than yourself.
PHILIPPIANS 2:3 TLB

During a trip, a young couple decided to take a tour of a cavern system. They were amazed as they began to notice the wonderful rock formations. The constant dripping sound served as a reminder that the marble-like pillars were formed over centuries of time by tiny drops of water.

A similar process goes on inside each of us. A single thought that finds its way into our minds leaves sediment that sinks deep down within our souls, forming our own pillars—pillars of character. If we let immoral, selfish, and violent thoughts fill our minds, we form eroding pillars of evil and failure. If we fill our minds with truth and love, we form strong and beautiful pillars within our souls.

> Here's the key of success and the key to failure: we become what we think about.

In Proverbs 23:7, King Solomon said, "For as he thinketh in his heart, so is he." Solomon understood that the things we dwell on determine the person we become. When we pursue God, we begin to reflect His character in our lives.

What formed the pillars of character in your life? Do you bear any resemblance to your Heavenly Father?

You can become the person God has designed you to be by renewing your mind daily in the Word of God. Just as the Carlsbad Caverns were developed over time, hidden from view, so our own true character is built.

Finally, brethren, whatsoever things are true, whatsoever things are honest . . . if there be any virtue, and if there be any praise, think on these things.
PHILIPPIANS 4:8

> Always bear in mind that your
> own resolution to success is more
> important than any other one thing.

Famous stage and film actress Helen Hayes believed her "resoluteness" about her own potential for success played an important role at the beginning of her career. She once said: "Before the authors gave me the script, they observed, in a matter-of-course manner, 'Of course you play piano? You'll have to sing to your own accompaniment in the piece.' As these alarming tidings were in the course of being made, I caught a bewildered look in my mother's eyes, and so I spoke up before she could. 'Certainly I play piano,' I answered.

"As we left the theater, my mother sighed, 'I hate to see you start under a handicap,' she said. 'What made you say you could play piano?' 'The feeling that I *will* play before rehearsals begin,' I said. We went at once to try to rent a piano . . . and ended by buying one. I began lessons at once, practiced finger exercises till I could no longer see the notes— and began rehearsals with the ability to accompany myself. Since then, I have never lived too far from a piano."

What you believe about your own potential for success counts far more than what any other person may believe. Believe what God believes about you—you were created for success.

The Lord God will help me; therefore shall I not be confounded: therefore have I set my face like a flint, and I know that I shall not be ashamed.

ISAIAH 50:7

Many years ago in England, a small boy grew up speaking with a lisp. He was never a scholar in school. And when war broke out involving his nation, he was rejected from service, told that "we need men." He once rose to address the House of Commons and all present walked out of the room. In fact, he often spoke to empty chairs and echoes. But one day he became Prime Minister of Great Britain, and with stirring speeches and bold decisions, he led his nation to victory. His name was Sir Winston Churchill.

Triumph is just "umph" added to try.

Many years ago in Illinois, a man with only a few years of formal education failed in business in '31, was defeated in a run for the state legislature in '32, again failed in business in '33, was elected to the legislature in '34, but defeated for speaker in '38. He was defeated for elector in '40, defeated for congress in '43, elected to congress in '46, but defeated in '48. He was defeated for senate in '55, defeated for the vice presidential nomination in '56, and defeated for the senate in '58. But in 1860, he was elected president. His name was Abraham Lincoln.

No one is defeated until he gives up trying.

Whatsoever thy hand findeth
to do, do it with thy might.
ECCLESIASTES 9:10

A goal properly set is
halfway reached.

A young man in need of work once saw this advertisement in a Boston newspaper: "Wanted, young man as an understudy to a financial statistician, P.O. Box 1720." The young man decided this was just the kind of job he wanted, so he replied to the ad but received no answer. He wrote again, and even a third time with no reply. Next, he went to the Boston post office and asked the name of the holder of Box 1720, but the clerk refused to give it, as did the postmaster.

Early one morning an idea came to the young man. He rose early, took the first train to Boston, went to the post office, and stood watch near Box 1720. After a while, a man appeared, opened the box, and took out the mail. The young man followed him as he returned to the office of a stock brokerage firm. The young man entered and asked for the manager.

In the interview, the manager asked, "How did you find out that I was the advertiser?" The young man told about his detective work, to which the manager replied, "Young man, you are just the kind of persistent fellow I want. You are employed!"

If a goal is worthy, there's no good reason to stop pursuing it! Find something you truly want to do, then go for it with all your heart, mind, and strength.

The LORD answered me, and said,
Write the vision, and make it plain upon
tables, that he may run that readeth it.
HABAKKUK 2:2

Henry P. Davison was a prominent American financier and one-time head of the American Red Cross. He worked his way up from being a poor boy to become president of a large New York City bank.

While he was a cashier of that bank, a would-be robber came to his window, pointed a revolver at him, and passed a check across his window counter. The check was for $1 million, payable to the Almighty. Davison remained calm, even though he realized the gravity of the situation. In a loud voice, he repeated the words on the check back to the person standing in front of him, emphasizing the "million dollars." Then he graciously asked the would-be robber how he would like to have *the million dollars* for the Almighty. He then proceeded to count

> I think the one lesson I have learned is that there is no substitute for paying attention.

out small bills. In the meantime, the suspicion of a guard had been aroused by the strange request he had overheard. He disarmed the robber and prevented the theft.

In later years, Davison was often asked to give his wisdom to others seeking success. He often advised that courtesy, readiness, willingness, and alertness do more for a person than being smart.

Therefore we ought to give the more earnest heed to the things which we have heard, lest any time we should let them slip.

HEBREWS 2:1

> **A good listener is not only popular everywhere, but after a while he knows something.**

An American Indian was once visiting New York City. As he walked the busy Manhattan streets with a friend from the city, he suddenly stopped, tilted his head to one side, and said, "I hear a cricket."

"You're crazy," his friend said. The Cherokee answered, "No, I hear a cricket, I do! I'm sure of it."

The friend replied, "It's the noon hour. People are jammed on the sidewalks, cars are honking, taxis are whizzing by, the city is full of noise. And you think you can hear a cricket?"

"I'm sure I do," said the visitor. He listened even more closely and then walked to the corner, spotted a shrub in a large cement planter, dug into the leaves underneath it, and pulled out a cricket. His friend was astounded. The man said, "The fact is, my friend, that my ears are different than yours. It all depends on what your ears have been tuned to hear. Let me show you." And at that, he reached into his pocket, pulled out a handful of loose change and dropped the coins on the pavement. Every head within a half block turned. "See what I mean?" he said, picking up the coins. "It all depends on what you are listening for."

Listen today to those things that will make you wise. Heed those things that prepare you for eternity.

The ear that heareth the reproof of life abideth among the wise.
PROVERBS 15:31

These words were spelled out in lights at the 18th Olympics in Tokyo: "The most important thing in the Olympic Games is not to win but to take part; just as the most important thing in life is not the triumph but the struggle. The essential thing is . . . to have fought well."

The athletes who make it to the Olympic Games are already the best of the best from each nation. Each athlete has excelled in ways few of his or her peers will ever know. And yet, at the Olympic Games, only one will wear a gold medal, one silver, and one bronze.

> You may be disappointed if you fail, but you are doomed if you don't try.

Those who are so accustomed to winning face the devastating possibility of losing before not only their teammates, but their countrymen, and in this age of world-wide television, before the entire world. How vital it is for these athletes to keep their perspective—that winning is not the important issue at the Olympics, but the opportunity to compete, to try, and to give one's best effort.

Regardless of the arena in which you compete, *winning* is not what is truly important. Giving your best effort to a challenge is what molds within you the lasting traits and character that are "better than gold."

The sluggard craves and gets nothing, but the desires of the diligent are fully satisfied.
PROVERBS 13:4 NIV

Success is never final;
failure is never fatal;
it is courage that counts.

In *The Seven Habits of Highly Effective People,* Stephen R. Covey writes: "One of the most inspiring times Sandra and I have ever had took place over a four-year period with a dear friend of ours named Carol, who had a wasting cancer disease. She had been one of Sandra's bridesmaids, and they had been best friends for over 25 years.

"When Carol was in the very last stages of the disease, Sandra spent time at her bedside helping her write her personal history. She returned from those protracted and difficult sessions almost transfixed by admiration for her friend's courage and her desire to write special messages to be given to her children at different stages in their lives.

"Carol would take as little pain-killing medication as possible, so that she had full access to her mental and emotional faculties. Then she would whisper into a tape recorder or to Sandra directly as she took notes. Carol was so proactive, so brave, and so concerned about others that she became an enormous source of inspiration to many people around her."

In today's world there is perhaps one trait that is needed desperately. Seek to develop it. It's called *courage.*

Be of good courage, and he
shall strengthen your heart,
all ye that hope in the LORD.
PSALM 31:24

A quiet forest dweller who lived high above an Austrian village in the Alps was hired by a town council to keep the pristine mountain springs, the source of the town's water supply, clear of debris. With faithful regularity, the old man patrolled the hills, clearing away silt and removing leaves and branches from the springs. Over time, the village became prosperous. Mill wheels turned, farms were irrigated, and tourists came. Years passed. Then, at a council meeting about the city budget, a member noticed the salary figure for the old man. He asked, "Who is he and why do we keep him on the payroll? Has anybody seen him? For all we know, he might be dead." The council voted to dispense with his services.

> I count him braver who overcomes his desires than he who conquers his enemies; for the hardest victory is the victory over self.

For several weeks nothing changed. Then the trees began to shed their leaves. One afternoon a town citizen noticed a brown tint to the water. Within another week, a slick covered sections of the canals and a foul odor was detected. Sickness broke out.

The town council called a special meeting and, reversing their error in judgment, rehired the old man. Renewed life soon returned to the village as the sparkling waters returned. What was the name of this keeper of the springs? He was called the Spirit of Self-Control.

I keep under my body, and
bring it into subjection.
1 CORINTHIANS 9:27

> ## Vision is the world's most desperate need. There are no hopeless situations— only people who think hopelessly.

One of the great disasters of history took place in 1271. In that year, Niccolo and Matteo Polo, the father and uncle of Marco Polo, visited the Kubla Khan, who was considered the world ruler—with authority over all China, all India, and all of the East.

The Kubla Khan was attracted to the story of Christianity as Niccolo and Matteo told it to him. He said to them, "You shall go to your high priest and tell him on my behalf to send me a hundred men skilled in your religion and I shall be baptized, and when I am baptized all my barons and great men will be baptized and their subjects will receive baptism, too, and so there will be more Christians here than there are in your parts."

Nothing was done, however, in response to what the Kubla Khan had requested. Only after thirty years were a handful of missionaries sent! Too few, too late.

The West apparently did not have the vision to see the East won to Christ. The mind boggles at the possible ways the world might be different today if thirteenth-century China, India, and the other areas of the Orient had become fully Christian.

If you lack vision today, ask God for it. He has wonders to reveal to you that you can't yet imagine!

*Where there is no vision,
the people perish.*
PROVERBS 29:18

Bishop Fulton Sheen, perhaps best known for his radio sermons on the "Catholic Hour" broadcast and his "Life Is Worth Living" weekly telecast, once recalled this as the most memorable experience in his life, a moment when he truly identified with Christ:

> The Supervisor's Prayer:
>
> Lord, when I am wrong, make me willing to change; when I am right, make me easy to live with. So strengthen me that the power of my example will far exceed the authority of my rank.

"I visited a leper colony in Africa. I brought with me 500 small silver crucifixes to give to each victim of the dread disease. The first leper who came up to me had only a stump of his left arm. . . . The right arm and hand were full of those telltale white open sores of leprosy. I held the crucifix a few inches above the hand and let it drop into the palm. At that moment there were 501 lepers in the camp, and the most leprous of them all was myself. I had taken the symbol of Redemption, of Divine Love for man . . . and had refused to identify myself with all that symbol implied. . . . Seeing myself in the full shame of refusing to identify myself with this victim, I looked at the crucifix in the putrid mass of his hand and realized that I, too, must become one with suffering humanity. Then I pressed my hand to his hand with the symbol of Love between us and continued to do it for the other 499 lepers."

"Let your light shine before men in such a way that they may see your good works, and glorify your Father who is in heaven."
MATTHEW 5:16

Give me a task too big, too hard for human hands,

then I shall come at length to lean on Thee,

and leaning, find my strength.

A physician told Jim Stovall at age seventeen the news he feared: he was losing his sight irreversibly. Rather than drop out of life, Jim pursued a college degree and also studied privately with a very successful entrepreneur. Jim's goal was to be in business for himself, even if blind, so he might manage his own career and life.

Even though he had prepared himself for blindness, when the day came that he could no longer see, Jim felt devastated. In his book, *You Don't Have to Be Blind to See,* he says, "All I wanted to do was sit in my living room in my familiar chair and listen to music." But then Jim dug deep into his faith and, as he says, "God opened my inner eyes to a new idea."

Jim entered a highly unusual field for a blind person—television! He founded the Narrative Television Network (NTN) to aid visually impaired people. NTN adds more "descriptive narration" to TV sound tracks so that listeners might visualize a program or movie and enjoy it more fully. As one of the fastest-growing networks ever, NTN boasts over 1,200 broadcast and cable affiliates, reaching 25 million homes in the U.S. and 11 foreign countries. For his work, Jim received television's highest honor, the Emmy Award, after only one season on the air.

Trust in the LORD with all your heart and lean not on your own understanding.
PROVERBS 3:5 NIV

Many people today seem to go through their days with their "stingers out," ready to attack others or to defend their positions at the slightest provocation. We all do well, however, to consider the full nature of the "bees" we sometimes seem to emulate.

Bees readily feed each other, sometimes even a bee of a different colony. The worker bees feed the queen bee, who cannot feed herself. They feed the drones during their period of usefulness in the hive. They feed the young. They seem to enjoy this social act of mutual feeding.

> The most important single ingredient in the formula of success is knowing how to get along with people.

Bees cluster together for warmth in cold weather and fan their wings to cool the hive in hot weather, thus working for one another's comfort.

When the time comes for bees to move to new quarters, scouts report back to the group, doing a dance very similar to the one used to report a find of honey. When enough scouts have confirmed the suitability of the new location, the bees appear to make a common decision, take wing, and migrate together—all at the same time—in what we call a swarm.

Only as a last resort of self-defense do bees engage their stingers, and then, never against their fellow bees. We do well to learn from them!

See that no one pays back evil
for evil, but always try to do good
to each other and to everyone else.
1 Thessalonians 5:15 tlb

> # Everyone thinks of changing the world, but no one thinks of changing himself.

Andrew Carnegie, considered to be one of the first to emphasize self-esteem and the potential for inner greatness, was famous for his ability to produce millionaires from among his employees. One day a reporter asked him, "How do you account for the fact you have 43 millionaires working for you?"

Carnegie replied, "They weren't rich when they came. We work with people the same way you mine gold. You have to remove a lot of dirt before you find a small amount of gold."

Andrew Carnegie knew how to bring about change in people. He helped them realize their hidden treasure within, inspired them to develop it, and then watched with encouragement as their lives became transformed.

The philosopher and psychologist William James once said, "Compared to what we ought to be, we are only half awake. We are making use of only a small part of our physical and mental resources. Stating the thing broadly, the human individual thus lives far within his limits. He possesses powers of various sports which he habitually fails to use." In other words, most people only develop a fraction of their abilities. Go for a bigger percentage in *your* life. Find the gold nuggets within!

Unless you change and become
like little children you will never
enter the kingdom of heaven.
MATTHEW 18:3 NIV

Several years ago a well-known television circus show developed an act involving Bengal tigers. The act was performed live before a large audience. One night, the tiger trainer went into the cage with several tigers and the door was routinely locked behind him. Spotlights flooded the cage and television cameras moved in close so the audience could see every detail as he skillfully put the tigers through their paces.

> Courage is resistance to fear, mastery of fear— not absence of fear.

In the middle of the performance, the worst happened: the lights went out. For nearly thirty long dark seconds, the trainer was locked in with the tigers in the darkness. With their superb night vision, the tigers could see him, but he could not see them. Still, he survived. And when the lights came on, he calmly finished his performance.

When the trainer was asked how he felt, he admitted to feeling chilling fear at first, but then, he said, he realized that even though he couldn't see the big cats, *they didn't know he couldn't see them.* He said, "I just kept cracking my whip and talking to them until the lights came on. They never knew I couldn't see them as well as they could see me."

Keep talking back to the tigers that seem to be stalking you. They *will* obey your voice of faith!

*Yea, though I walk through the
valley of the shadow of death, I will
fear no evil: for thou art with me;
thy rod and thy staff they comfort me.*

PSALM 23:4

> Prayer is an invisible tool which
> is wielded in a visible world.

Both a major thoroughfare in Tel Aviv and a bridge that spans the Jordan River are named in honor of Viscount Edmund Henry Hynman Allenby, a British soldier. As commander of the Egyptian Expeditionary Forces, he outwitted and defeated the Turks in Palestine in 1917 and 1918, conquering Jerusalem without ever firing a single gun.

As a British soldier, Allenby was noncommittal about the official British policies concerning the establishment of a Jewish National Home, but he did have a deep understanding of the Jews' desire to dwell in Palestine. At a reception in London, he once told how, as a little boy, he had knelt to say his evening prayers, repeating with his childhood lisp the words his mother prayed: "And, O Lord, we would not forget Thine ancient people, Israel; hasten the day when Israel shall again be Thy people and shall be restored to Thy favor and to their land."

Allenby concluded, "I never knew then that God would give me the privilege of helping to answer my own childhood prayers."

What you pray today may very well be part of tomorrow's work. The world you envision in prayer may very well be the world in which you one day live!

The weapons of our warfare are not carnal, but mighty through God to the pulling down of strong holds.
2 CORINTHIANS 10:4

A strange memorial can be found in the Mount Hope Cemetery of Hiawatha, Kansas. John M. Davis, an orphan, developed a strong dislike for his wife's family and insisted that none of his fortune go to them. He also refused requests that he eventually bequeath his estate for a hospital desperately needed in the area. Instead, after his wife died in 1930, Mr. Davis chose to invest in an elaborate tomb for himself and his wife. The tomb includes a number of statues depicting the couple at various stages of their lives. One statue is of Mr. Davis as a lonely man seated beside an empty chair titled "the vacant chair." Another shows him placing a wreath in front of his wife's tombstone. Many of the statues are made of Kansas granite. No money was left for the memorial's upkeep.

Money is like an arm or leg: use it or lose it.

Today, largely because of its weight, this costly memorial is slowly sinking into the ground. It has become weathered and worn from the strong winds in this plains state. The townspeople regard the Davis tomb as an "old man's folly," and many predict that within the next fifty years, the memorial will have become obliterated beyond recognition and will need to be demolished. What could have been a living legacy will eventually become granite dust.

"To him who has will more be given . . . and he will have great plenty; but for him who has not, even the little he has will be taken away."

MATTHEW 13:12 TLB

283

Men will spend their health getting wealth, then gladly pay all they have earned to get health back.

As former campaign manager for President George Bush and chairman of the Republican National Committee, Lee Atwater had accomplished the two things he had wanted to do by the time he was 40. Then he was diagnosed with a malignant brain tumor. Shortly before he died, he wrote: "I acquired more than most. But you can acquire all you want and still feel empty. What power wouldn't I trade for a little more time with my family? What price wouldn't I pay for an evening with friends? It took a deadly illness to put me eye to eye with that truth, but it is a truth the country can learn on my dime.

"I lie here in my bedroom, my face swollen from steroids, my body useless. The doctors still won't answer that nagging question: how long do I have? Some nights I can't go to sleep, so fearful am I that I will never wake up again.

"I've come a long way since the day I told George Bush that his 'kinder, gentler' theme was a nice thought, but it wouldn't win us any votes. I used to say that the president might be kinder and gentler, but I wasn't going to be. How wrong I was. There is nothing more important in life than human beings, nothing sweeter than the human touch."

What will it profit a man if he gains the whole world and forfeits his life?
MATTHEW 16:26 AMP

When Chief Justice Charles Evans Hughes moved to Washington, D.C., to take up his duties on the Supreme Court, he transferred his church membership letter to a Baptist church in the area.

It was customary for all new members in this church to come to the front of the sanctuary at the close of the worship service so they might be officially introduced and welcomed. The first person to be called forward that morning was Ah Sing, a Chinese laundryman who had moved to Washington from the West Coast. He took his place at the far side of the church. As the dozen or so others were called forward that day, they came forward and stood on the opposite side of the church, leaving Ah Sing standing alone.

> Let us not say,
> Every man is the
> architect of his own
> fortune; but let us say,
> Every man is the archi-
> tect of his own character.

Finally Chief Justice Hughes was called forward, and he immediately made his way to the front and proceeded to stand next to Ah Sing. The minister who welcomed the group into church fellowship said, "I do not want this congregation to miss this remarkable illustration of the fact that at the cross of Jesus Christ the ground is level."

Your choice of friends will greatly influence the manner in which your character develops. So, too, will your choice of those whom you befriend.

Till I die I will not remove mine integrity
from me. My righteousness I hold fast,
and will not let it go: my heart shall
not reproach me so long as I live.
JOB 27:5-6

> It is impossible for that man to
> despair who remembers that
> his Helper is omnipotent.

E. Stanley Jones tells the story of a missionary who became lost in an African jungle.
Looking around, he saw nothing but bush and
a few clearings. He stumbled about until he
finally came across a native hut. He asked one
of the natives if he could lead him out of the
jungle and back to the mission station. The
native agreed to help him.

"Thank you!" exclaimed the missionary.
"Which way do I go?" The native replied,
"Walk." And so they did, hacking their way
through the unmarked jungle for more than
an hour.

In pausing to rest, the missionary looked
around and had the same overwhelming sense
that he was lost. All he saw was bush and a

few clearings. "Are you quite sure this is the way?" he asked. "I don't see any path."

The native looked at him and replied, "Bwana, in this place there is no path. I am the path."

When we have no clues, we must remember that God who guides us is omniscient—all wise. When we feel lonely, we must remember that God is omnipresent—all places at the same time. When we are weak, we must remember that God is omnipotent—all powerful.

I will lift up my eyes to the mountains;
from where shall my help come?
My help comes from the LORD,
who made the heaven and earth.
PSALM 121:1-2 NASB

Former cohost of *Good Morning America,* Joan Lunden recalls, "When I first came on [the] program in 1978, hosting with David Hartman, he got to interview all the celebrities and politicians and kings. I got the information spots. . . . I received piles of letters from women who were unhappy that I was allowing myself to be used this way. Well, the fact was, I enjoyed those spots and I was good at them. I had to accept that it was either that way or no way at all. I got very good advice from Barbara Walters, who said: 'Joan, don't buck city hall or you're gonna end up where all your female predecessors ended up—out there somewhere. Do the absolute best with what they give you and make those little morsels shine. And then go out and make the

> The price of success is hard work, dedication to the job at hand, and determination that whether we win or lose, we have applied the best of ourselves to the task at hand.

bigger interviews happen on your own.' That's how I approached the job.

"I can't see any reason to spend your time frustrated, angry, or upset about things you don't have or you can't have or you can't yet do. I drill this into my children when I hear them say, 'I don't have this.' And I'll say, 'Don't focus on what you don't have. Focus on what you do have and be grateful for it. Be proud of what you can do. Those things you can't do yet, maybe you will do.'"

Whatsoever ye do, do it heartily,
as to the Lord, and not unto men.
COLOSSIANS 3:23

> Those that have done nothing in life are not qualified to judge those that have done little.

In the 1700s, an English cobbler kept a map of the world on his workshop wall so that he might be reminded to pray for the nations of the world. As the result of such prayer, he became especially burdened for a specific missionary outreach. He shared this burden at a meeting of ministers, but was told by a senior minister, "Young man, sit down. When God wants to convert the heathen, He will do it without your help or mine."

The cobbler, William Carey, did not let this man's remarks put out the flame of his concern. When he couldn't find others to support the missionary cause that had burdened his soul, he became a missionary himself. His pioneering efforts in India are legendary, with many recording mighty exploits for God.

Be careful in how you respond to the enthusiasm of others that you don't dampen a zeal for God. Be cautious in how you respond to the new ideas of another that you don't squelch God-given creativity.

Be generous and kind in evaluating the work of others so that you might encourage those things which are worthy. Be slow to judge and quick to praise. And pray for the same in your own life!

*"Judge not, and ye shall not
be judged: condemn not, and
ye shall not be condemned."*
LUKE 6:37

A young man once came to Jesus asking Him what he needed to do to have eternal life. Jesus replied that he should keep the commandments. The young man then claimed that he had always kept them. Jesus advised, "If you would be perfect, sell everything you have, give the money to the poor, and come and follow me" (Matthew 19:21).

> People, places, and things were never meant to give us life. God alone is the author of a fulfilling life.

The Scriptures tell us that the young man went away "sorrowful: for he had great possessions" (vs. 22). The young man not only had great possessions, but apparently those possessions had him! He couldn't bear to part with earthly, temporary goods in order to obtain heavenly, eternal goods. Jesus also taught, of course, that heaven's "wealth" can be ours now. This young man didn't have to wait until he died to attain the benefits of eternal life. If he had been willing to give up his hold on his "stuff," he could have enjoyed great joy, peace, and fulfillment in his life—apparently things he was lacking and seeking.

Take a look at your possessions today. Are there books, tapes, or clothes you can give away to someone in need of learning, inspiration, or clothing? Discover how rewarding giving can be.

"I am come that they might have life, and that they might have it more abundantly."
JOHN 10:10

COMMON

COURTESIES

FOR STUDENTS

*Treat others the same way you
want them to treat you.*
LUKE 6:31 NASB

We often refer to courtesy as "common courtesy," but it is far from common. In fact, courtesy is rare these days. How many people do you know who follow the very basic common courtesies given in this section?

A father once remarked about his three children: "My children may not be the brightest children in their class. They may not be the most talented or the most skilled. They may not achieve great fame, or earn millions of dollars. But by my insisting that they have good manners, I know they will be welcome in all places and by all people." How true!

Good manners—exhibiting common courtesies—are like a calling card. They open doors that are otherwise shut to those who are rude, crude, or unmannerly. They bring welcome invitations, and quite often, return engagements. They cover a multitude of weaknesses and flaws. They make other people feel good about themselves, and they in turn extend kindness and generosity they might not otherwise exhibit. Good manners are a prerequisite for good friendships, good business associations, and good marriages. They are a key to success.

Which virtuous behaviors on earth will still be required in Heaven?

Courage? No. There will be nothing to fear in Heaven.

Hope? No. We will have all that we desire.

Faith? No. We will be in the presence of the Source of our faith, and all those things for which we have believed will have their fulfillment in Him and by His hand.

Acts of charity toward those in need? No. There will be no hunger, thirst, nakedness, or homelessness in Heaven. All needs will be supplied.

Sympathy? No, for there will be no more tears and no more pain.

Courtesy? Yes! There will still be room for the exercise of courtesy, the kind greeting, the

> 1.
> Always say please, thank you, and excuse me.

simple manners that offend no one but ease the way of all.

Good manners help win friends. They please others. Good manners help put people at ease, which in turn makes them more cooperative and happy. Immanuel Kant once said, "Always treat a human being as a person, that is, as an end in himself, and not merely as a means to your end." Strive to impart dignity and self-worth to all you meet. Consider it dress rehearsal for a future life in Heaven.

His merciful kindness is great toward us:
and the truth of the Lord endureth forever.
Praise ye the Lord!
PSALM 117:2

2.

Always knock and ask permission before entering someone's room.

A mother watched with raised eyebrows as her two sons took a hammer and a few nails from the kitchen utility drawer and scurried to one of the boys' rooms, giggling and talking in low voices. When she didn't hear any hammering, she continued with her chores. Then from the kitchen window she saw one of the boys take a stepladder from the garage. He disappeared from sight before she could call to him. A few minutes later her other son came into the kitchen to ask if she had any rope. "No," Mom said. "What's going on?" Her son said, "Nothin'." Mom pressed, "Are you sure?" but her son was out of sight.

Highly suspicious, Mom went to her older son's room. She found the door closed and locked. She knocked. "What are you boys doing in there?" she asked. One son replied, "Nothin'." Suspecting great mischief she demanded entrance, "I want you to open this door right now!" she said. A few seconds later the door popped open and one son shouted, "Surprise!" as he handed her a rather crudely wrapped present. "Happy birthday, Mom!" the other boy added. Truly surprised, the mother stammered, "But what about the hammer, nails, ladder, and rope?" The boys grinned, "Those were just decoys, Mom."

As those who have been chosen of God, holy and beloved, put on a heart of compassion, kindness, humility, gentleness and patience.

COLOSSIANS 3:12 NASB

While driving down a country road, a man came to a very narrow bridge. In front of the bridge a sign was posted. It read, "Yield." Seeing no oncoming cars, he continued across the bridge and to his destination. On his way back this same route, he came to the same one-lane bridge, now from the opposite direction. To his surprise, he saw another "Yield" sign posted there.

Curious, he thought. *I'm sure there was one posted on the other side.* Sure enough, when he reached the other side of the bridge and looked back, he saw the sign. Yield signs had been placed at both ends of the bridge, obviously with the intent that drivers from both directions were requested to give each other the right of way. It was a reasonable and doubly sure way to prevent a head-on collision.

3.

Show respect to anyone in authority.

If you find yourself in a combative situation with someone who has more authority than you—or equal authority in a particular situation—it is always wise to yield to them. If they indeed have *more* authority, a lack of submission will put you in a position to be punished or reprimanded. If you are of equal authority, an exercise of your power will only build resentment in a person better kept as an ally.

We ask you, brothers, to respect those who work hard among you, who are over you in the Lord and who admonish you.
1 THESSALONIANS 5:12 NIV

4.
Always RSVP promptly to every invitation you receive.

The letters RSVP stand for the French phrase *résponde vous s'il vous plait*—"please respond." This phrase on an invitation asks that you let the host or hostess know whether you plan to attend the function. Every invitation marked with RSVP requires that you call or write the host to let them know that you either will or will not be there.

Occasionally a handwritten invitation will say, "RSVP, regrets only." In this case, you are required to notify the host only if you will *not* be attending. However, truly thoughtful guests who plan to attend will call or mail a note to the host to thank him for the invitation and confirm that they will attend.

Imagine that you planned a catered party for fifty guests and you were paying $25 per guest. Then imagine that half your guests failed to respond and ten of them did not show up. You would be spending $250 for people who simply were not considerate enough to let you know that they could not be present. Would you consider those people to be thoughtful friends?

Be the kind of guest that you would like to have attend your own fanciest party!

Who among you is wise and understanding?
Let him show by his good behavior his
deeds in the gentleness of wisdom.
JAMES 3:13 NASB

A store once had this lay-away policy: "We hold it in the store while you pay for it. You're mad. You take it from the store and don't pay for it. We're mad. Better that you're mad." Mark Twain's neighbor may have had this policy in mind when Twain asked to borrow a certain book he had spotted in his neighbor's library. "Why, yes, Mr. Clemens, you're more than welcome to it," the neighbor said. "But I must ask you to read it here. You know I make it a rule never to let a book go out of my library."

Several days later the neighbor came to Twain's house and asked if he could borrow his lawn mower since his had been taken to the repair shop. "Why, certainly," the humorist replied. "You're more than welcome to it. But I must

5.
Return anything borrowed on time, and in good condition.

ask you to use it only in my yard. You know I make it a rule."

Treat what you borrow as if it was a prized possession and return it promptly. If something happens to it while it is in your possession, make repairs or replace it, not to your satisfaction, but to the satisfaction of the owner. Always remember, while the item is in your hands, it is *not* yours. It still belongs to the other person.

The integrity of the upright shall guide them.
PROVERBS 11:3

6.

Be on time for appointments;
leave on time, too, for nothing is more boring
than someone who overstays his welcome.

Mr. Brown was in his final year of seminary, preparing to become a pastor. The policy of his school called for him to be available at a moment's notice to fill in for local churches who might need a preacher. Mr. Brown eagerly awaited such an opportunity, and at long last, his moment arrived. The pastor of a country church was called away on an emergency and he was asked to fill the pulpit.

Having waited so long for the opportunity, and having so much to say, Mr. Brown soon became completely immersed in his own words. The more he preached, the more he became inspired to preach. When he glanced at his watch he was shocked to see that he had preached for a full hour. He was truly embarrassed since he had been allotted only thirty minutes to preach. Knowing that he had preached well into the lunch hour, he made a heartfelt apology to the congregation and sat down.

A young woman hurried to him after the service ended. Obviously more impressed with his personality and appearance—and perhaps his availability—than she was with his message, she gushed, "Oh, Brother Brown, you needn't have apologized. You really didn't talk long—it just seemed long."

Let everyone see that you are unselfish
and considerate in all you do.
PHILIPPIANS 4:5 TLB

Walter Slezak was pleasantly surprised to see his teenage daughter answer the telephone and then hang up after talking for only twenty minutes, instead of her usual hour. Sllezak congratulated her for keeping the conversation so brief and asked which of her friends had cooperated. "That wasn't a friend," she said. "It was a wrong number."

Everyone misdials a number now and then. But you can keep down your own frustration level and help others to have a nicer day, too, when you do the following:

> 7.
>
> When you dial a wrong number, say, "I'm sorry, excuse me"—instead of slamming down the receiver in the other person's ear.

Be sure you have dialed a number other than the one you intended to call. Ask the person on the other end of the line, "Could you tell me if I have dialed [stating the number you intended to dial]?" The answer may keep you from ringing the same number again and causing a person further interruption. It will also help you discover if you have the correct phone number for the person you are trying to reach.

Once you have established that you have reached a wrong number, say, "I'm sorry to have bothered you," or a similar polite response.

Be kind to those, too, who call you by mistake. Don't let an interruption turn into aggravation.

You, Lord, are good and ready to forgive,
And abundant in lovingkindness
to all who call upon You.
PSALM 86:5 NASB

8.
Never cheat on your place in line.

A newly elected politician had just arrived in Washington, D.C. He was eager to meet his colleagues and to discover the inner workings of the government. Shortly after his arrival, he was invited to the home of a senior senator. He waited until they were alone together on his deck, overlooking the Potomac River, and then he asked, "How does the power *really* flow in this city?"

The senator thought for a moment and then pointed toward an old deteriorating log floating by on the river below them. He said, "This city is like that log out there." The fledgling politician asked, "How so?" The old-timer came back, "Well there are probably more than a hundred thousand grubs, ants, bugs, and other critters riding on that old log as it floats down the river. And imagine every one of them thinks that he's steering it."

Many of us—thinking ourselves or our time more important than that of others—try to cheat on our place in lines, including snaking through traffic lanes during rush hour and giving ourselves special "privileges." Most of the time, these are not acts of prudence, but of pride. Keep your place, and you'll likely find you also keep your peace.

In all things show yourself to be
an example of good deeds, with
purity in doctrine, dignified.
Titus 2:7 NASB

The story is told of a mother who had raised six boys to manhood. Her work never done, she had finally taken to her sickbed in utter exhaustion. Each of the boys came home to see his mother as she lay on her deathbed. Her oldest son, a powerful and great man, knelt by her bedside and, wiping her forehead, said to her, "Mother, you have always been a good mother to us boys."

The weary woman closed her eyes and giant tears pushed out under the lids and ran down her hollow cheeks. Then she opened her eyes and said to her son, "My boy, I prayed more that I might be a good mother to you six boys than for anything else. I was afraid that I should fail in some way to be all that I ought to be for you, and I never knew whether you boys thought I had failed or not

9.

Learn how to pay compliments. Start with the members of your family, and you will find it will become easier in life to compliment others. It's a great asset.

until now. Not one of you ever told me I was a good mother until today."

When was the last time you told a parent, grandparent, or other adult how much you appreciate all that he or she has done for you? When was the last time you complimented or gave an expression of value to a brother or sister? Don't delay. The time may come when you no longer have the opportunity.

Bless those who persecute you;
bless and do not curse.
ROMANS 12:14 NASB

10.
Don't put your feet up on the furniture. Feet do not enhance the look of the desk or the table.

A very cunning fox had a stork for a neighbor. He desired to keep on very friendly terms with her, thinking that one day she might build a nest and deposit eggs for him to steal and devour. Toward that end, he always treated the stork with a great deal of kind attention. Whenever he saw her out in public, he paid her many compliments. He decided the ultimate kindness he might show her would be to invite her to dinner. Being stingy, however, he prepared soup for dinner, and he served this on a shallow plate. The fox, of course, could easily lap up the soup with his broad tongue, but the stork, with her long narrow bill, was hardly able to eat a drop.

The fox laughed to himself when she was gone . . . but not for long. Soon after, the stork invited him to a dinner party and she, too, served soup. But she served it in a bottle!

Always take your cues for manners from your host or hostess. Don't help yourself to anything they don't offer or make yourself more "at home" than they do. While you are in *their* home or office, their manners—not yours—are the rule.

While we have opportunity,
let us do good to all men.
GALATIANS 6:10 NIV

Acknowledgments

We acknowledge and thank the following people for the quotes used in this book: Syrus (10), Dr. Eugene Swearingen (14,32,36), Gary Smalley and John Trent (16,294), Harry Emerson Fosdick (18,204), Calvin Coolidge (20,210), David Shibley (24), Bill Copeland (26), Les Brown (28), John D. Rockefeller, Jr. (30), Thomas Jefferson (34,116), Robert C. Edward (38), Ed Cole (40,64,280), Benjamin Franklin (42,224), Kin Hubbard (48), Henry Ward Beecher (50,246), John A. Shedd (54), Ralph Waldo Emerson (58,160), Dwight L. Moody (60), H.E. Jansen (66), A.W. Tozer (74), Roy Disney (76), Descartes (78), Helen Keller (80), Seneca (82), Aristotle (84,162,266), Matthew Prior (86), Dwight L. Moody (88), William A. Ward (90), Katherine Graham (92), Moliere (96), Bob Bales (98), Solon (100), Charles C. Noble (102), Samuel Johnson (104,292), Eleanor Roosevelt (106), John Sculley (108), George Bernard Shaw (110), Oprah Winfrey (112), Franklin (120), Woodrow Wilson (122), Charles H. Spurgeon (124), William Lyon Phelps (126), Washington Irving (128), Terence (132), Henry Wadsworth Longfellow (144), Josh Billings (146), Jean Paul Richter (150), William James (152), Samuel Butler (154), H.P. Liddon (156), George Elliot (158), John R. Rice (164). William H. Danforth (166,186,220), Thomas A. Edison (168), Battista (170), George Edward Woodberry (172), Ronald E. Osborn (174), Bill Cosby (176), Winston Churchill (178,264), Thomas Carlyle (182), Bacon (184), Lillian Dickson (188), Denis Diderot (190), Earl Nightingale (192,250), Horace (194), Louis D. Brandeis (196), Hannah More (198), Publilius Syrus (200), Orlando A. Battista (202), Victor Hugo (206), David Dunn (208), Mark Twain (212,278), Roy L. Smith (213), Phil Marquart (216), Oliver Wendell Holmes (218), George Washington (222), Andre Maurois (228), George Sala (230), Say (232), Cervantes (234), Ben Patterson (240), James Whitcomb Riley (242, 252), Zig Ziglar (244,256), Builder (248), Diane Sawyer (258), Wilson Mizner (260), Beverly Sills (262), Winifred Newman (268), Pauline H. Peters (270), Witt Fowler (272), Theodore Roosevelt (274), Leo Tolstoy (276), Henry Ford (282), Mike Murdock (284), George Dana Boardman (286), Jeremy Taylor (288), and Vince Lombardi (290).

Additional copies of this book and other titles in the
God's Little Devotional Book series are
available from your local bookstore.
Also look for our special gift editions in this series.

God's Little Devotional Book for Dad's
God's Little Devotional Book for Graduates
God's Little Devotional Book for Men
God's Little Devotional Book for Moms
God's Little Devotional Book for Teachers
God's Little Devotional Book for Teens
God's Little Devotional Book for Women

If you have enjoyed this book, or if it has impacted
your life,
we would like to hear from you.
Please contact us at:
Honor Books
An Imprint of Cook Communications Ministries
4050 Lee Vance View
Colorado Springs, CO 80918

Or by email at cookministries.com